Strategic Employee Surveys

Strategic
Employee Surveys

Jack W. Wiley

JOSSEY-BASS
A Wiley Imprint
www.josseybass.com

Published by Jossey-Bass
A Wiley Imprint
989 Market Street, San Francisco, CA 94103-1741—www.josseybass.com

Jossey-Bass books and products are available through most bookstores. To contact Jossey-Bass directly call our Customer Care Department within the U.S. at 800-956-7739, outside the U.S. at 317-572-3986, or fax 317-572-4002.

Jossey-Bass also publishes its books in a variety of electronic formats. Some content that appears in print may not be available in electronic books.

Library of Congress Cataloging-in-Publication Data

Wiley, Jack, date.
　　Strategic employee surveys / by Jack Wiley.
　　　　p.　cm.
　　Includes bibliographical references and index.
　　ISBN 978-0-470-88970-1 (hardback); 978-0-470-89095-0 (ebk);
　　978-0-470-89110-0 (ebk); 978-0-470-89111-7 (ebk)
　　　　1. Employee attitude surveys.　2. Organizational effectiveness—Evaluation.
　　3. Strategic planning.　I. Title.
　　HF5549.5A83 W55　2010
　　658.3'140723—dc22

2010020673

Printed in the United States of America
FIRST EDITION
HB Printing　　10 9 8 7 6 5 4 3 2 1

Contents

Figures and Tables

Figures

Tables

I dedicate this book to Mom and to the loving memory of Dad, parents not blessed with the same opportunities they made sure to provide their children.

Preface

This book deals with the subject of how to think about designing and implementing an employee survey program. I draw the ideas presented from my thirty-five years of experience of doing this work. During that time frame, I have supported organizations in almost all major industries and in most of the major economies around the world. For several years, I have wanted to record my ideas about the employee survey process and how to ensure its effectiveness, but it was not until 2002 that I developed the Strategic Survey Model. The model gave me the framework needed for organizing my thoughts and observations.

As both a researcher and a practitioner, I know the employee survey process can be a very powerful tool for organization development. In essence, this book speaks to the two elements of a survey program that most differentiate between successful and unsuccessful initiatives, the two elements that most impinge on the power of an employee survey process to bring about desired change. The first of these elements is the survey instrument itself. Does the instrument truly measure what is important to an organization's leadership? If it does, leadership will be interested in using the views of employees to drive change and strengthen the organization. If it does not, the survey results will provoke a "so what and who cares" reaction. Under those circumstances, nothing or very little will happen because the survey did not measure what was important and did not energize management to take action. I devote the first part of the book to reviewing why organizations conduct surveys and especially to connecting survey purpose to the overarching strategy of the organization. I present examples of how to measure most of the major topics found in employee surveys today.

The survey feedback and follow-up process is the second element that most distinguishes between successful and unsuccessful survey initiatives. Organizations should think through very carefully the process for how they will use the results of a survey, and this should occur well in advance of the launch of the survey itself. The survey feedback and action planning process is like a tool in the hands of a carpenter. Even a skilled carpenter does not master the use of a tool the first time he or she picks it up. The same is true for organizations. It takes practice to achieve proficiency in the use of the survey feedback and action planning process to drive change. Even so, the thoughtful organization can sidestep some pitfalls. Part Two of the book is devoted to laying out a time-tested and proven approach to survey feedback and action planning. I identify key pitfalls to avoid and offer suggestions for how to maximize the power of the follow-up process to strengthen the organization.

This book is not about the details of running a survey program. There are several good books available on this topic. Certainly, the lack of effective project planning can hamper if not destroy a survey initiative. One should never underestimate the importance of using sound judgment in the overall management of a survey project. This book, however, is about what I believe are the higher-order decisions: ensuring the survey program supports business strategy, that what gets measured by the survey instrument matters, and using the survey results to make lasting improvements.

Acknowledgments

There are several colleagues and coworkers to whom I am indebted. Four served as my most important mentors and had the greatest impact on my career and my way of thinking about employee surveys. The first is Rensis Likert, a patient colleague who took time, late in his career, to help a fledgling survey practitioner understand the power of the survey feedback and action planning process. The second is Walter Tornow, my supervisor at Control Data Corporation, who gave me my first opportunity to run a company-wide survey program and who cheered my efforts to place its survey results into a business framework that would resonate with our leadership team. The third is David Sirota, a survey practitioner par excellence, who guided my early thinking about what to measure in an employee survey and how to use survey results to drive organization change. The fourth is Benjamin Schneider, who taught all of us within the survey profession about how to integrate employee survey results with important measures of organizational success, especially measures of customer satisfaction.

On a day-to-day basis, there are many coworkers, both past and present, from whom I have learned. They represent some of the finest survey practitioners our field has to offer and include Scott Brooks, Bruce Campbell, Bill Erickson, Jeff Jolton, Stephanie Kendall, Kyle Lundby, Jeff Saltzman, and Sara Weiner. In the development of this book, and particularly in the quoting of norms-based research, I am grateful to my fellow researchers within the Kenexa Research Institute,

Anne Herman and Brenda Kowske. For supporting the book in an overall sense, I am thankful to several Kenexa executives including Mike Dolen, Jim Donoho, Troy Kanter, Rudy Karsan, Eric Lochner, and Sarah Teten. I was able to complete this book because of the corporate support they provided. Finally, I am indebted to two coworkers who worked side by side with me in the development and editing of this book from beginning to end, Jennifer Meyer and Kara Ruder.

The Author

Jack W. Wiley, Ph.D., is founder and executive director of the Kenexa Research Institute. Dr. Wiley is recognized internationally for groundbreaking research that links employee survey results to measures of customer satisfaction and business performance. He is also the creator of WorkTrends, an international survey research program that produces results featured in both scholarly studies and the popular press worldwide. He has more than thirty years of experience consulting with organizations in the health care, financial services, manufacturing, and retail industries.

Dr. Wiley has written several articles and book chapters and has made numerous presentations to professional associations around the world. He was elected Fellow in the Society for Industrial and Organizational Psychology, the American Psychological Association, and the Association for Psychological Science, and serves on the board of directors of the Human Resources Planning Society. Wiley holds a doctorate in organizational psychology from the University of Tennessee, is a licensed consulting psychologist, and has received accreditation as a senior professional in human resources (SPHR). Prior to joining Kenexa in 2006, Dr. Wiley was the founder and CEO of Gantz Wiley Research, a survey research consulting firm specializing in employee and customer surveys for international corporate clients.

Strategic Employee Surveys

Part One

Survey Design

Chapter One

Introduction

A properly developed and implemented employee survey system can be one of the most powerful tools available to management for assessing the effectiveness of its strategy and maximizing the potential of its human capital (Schiemann and Morgan, 2006). Employees, when asked questions that are well designed, provide answers that are clear and direct and that leaders can use to understand a wide range of issues facing their organization. This is because most employees are keen observers of their work environment, want to be part of a successful organization, and are looking for ways to make their voices heard. An employee survey can be an effective method for capturing such information and can serve as the foundation for bringing about change that will position the organization for greater success in the future.

About WorkTrends

For more than twenty-five years, Kenexa, a global provider of business solutions for human resources, has regularly conducted surveys among a representative sample of the U.S. workforce. The data from this survey program, known as WorkTrends, serve multiple purposes: they allow Kenexa to explore a number of important topics about work from the worker's point of view and convert those conclusions into findings that can be broadly shared through press releases, technical reports, and scientific articles. These data also allow Kenexa to compare the results of a given client's survey to a country-level workforce as a whole, specific industry sectors, or best practices organizations.

The primary data set used for the analyses presented in this book was collected in 2009 from workers in Brazil, Canada, China, France, Germany, India, Italy, Japan, Russia, Saudi Arabia, Spain, the United Arab Emirates, the United Kingdom, and the United States. These fourteen countries represent the twelve largest economies as measured by gross domestic product (GDP), accounting for 73 percent of the world's GDP (International Monetary Fund, 2009), as well as two important Middle Eastern economies: Saudi Arabia and the United Arab Emirates.

WorkTrends is a multitopic survey completed online by a sample of workers screened to match a country's worker population in terms of industry mix, job type, gender, age, and other key organizational and demographic variables. Those who work full time in organizations of one hundred employees or more are allowed to take the survey. The survey has 115 items that cover a wide range of workplace issues, such as managerial and leadership effectiveness, organizational values, policies and practices, and job satisfaction. In 2009, approximately twenty-two thousand workers completed the survey.

Employee surveys have been used for decades to help leadership teams understand how workers perceive the organization's policies and the effectiveness of supervision and management, rate their job satisfaction and their overall satisfaction with the employer, and describe the emphasis they see placed on such values as training, innovation and customer service. Higgs and Ashworth (1996) observe that over the past seventy years, the goals and methods of employee surveying have evolved. In the 1930s and 1940s, particularly in the United States, surveys were conducted to identify groups of workers with low morale who might be susceptible to attempts to organize them into unions. Over the next several decades, Higgs and Ashworth say, the more common use of employee surveys was to measure employee satisfaction and use the survey results for improving worker productivity. In the past twenty years, surveys have emphasized quality-of-life issues, benefits, work/life balance, diversity, and other "employer-of-choice" topics, that is, topics related to attracting and retaining employees. This is a result of an increased focus on both the costs and challenges of employee recruitment and retention. And in the most recent past, the trend in employee surveying has been to link both survey content and survey results to business strategy and business performance.

The use of surveys, particularly in large organizations, has become common. Research summarized by Allen Kraut (2006) reveals that almost three of every four large firms survey their employees. Kenexa's research in the United States supports Kraut's implication that surveys are more common in large organizations. Using WorkTrends, I found that exactly 50 percent of organizations with populations between 100 and 249 employees conducted an employee survey in the previous two years, whereas 72 percent of organizations with more than 10,000 employees had done so. Trend research conducted in the United States would also support the contention that employee surveying is becoming even more common. In 1993, 50 percent of all organizations of more than 100 employees conducted surveys. By 2009, that percentage had jumped to 60 percent.

A more global review of recent survey activity reveals that employers in many countries rely on this technique to help their leaders manage their businesses (see Table 1.1). Although the employee survey technique is not yet common in some countries around the world (for example, Saudi Arabia), five of the

Table 1.1 Survey Utilization Rate by Country

Low Utilization (34%–49%)	Medium Utilization (50%–59%)	High Utilization (60%–72%)
• France	• Brazil	• Canada
• Italy	• Germany	• China
• Japan		• India
• Russia		• United Kingdom
• Saudi Arabia		• United States
• Spain		
• United Arab Emirates		

fourteen countries studied show high use (60 percent or higher) of the employee survey technique. This includes two of the fast-emerging major economies: China and India.

Analyses of this same study also reveal that the occurrence of employee surveys varies widely by industry (see Table 1.2). Employee survey activity is the highest in the banking (67 percent), health care services and high-tech manufacturing (62 percent), and financial services industries (61 percent). In these sectors, where institutional knowledge and employee retention are highly valued, employees are considered essential to the organization's brand, and the firm's human capital is indeed viewed as a pivot point (Boudreau and Ramstad, 2007). Employee survey activity is the lowest in the light manufacturing and restaurants and bars (44 percent), and construction and engineering (45 percent) industries. These industries, with the exception of the engineering segment of the engineering and construction industry, are often characterized by higher turnover and lower educational and training requirements. Falling in the middle are many highly regulated industries such as transportation services, government, and education.

Table 1.2 Survey Utilization Rate by Industry

Low Utilization (40%–49%)	Medium Utilization (50–59%)	High Utilization (60–69%)
• Accounting and legal	• Business services	• Banking services
• Agriculture	• Communication and utilities services	• Financial services
• Construction and engineering	• Education	• Health care services
• Heavy manufacturing	• Food—wholesale and retail	• High-tech manufacturing
• Light manufacturing	• Government	
• Personal services	• Health care products	
• Restaurants and bars	• Hotel and lodging	
	• Mining	
	• Retail (nonfood)	
	• Transportation services	

As Kraut (2006) noted, the popularity of surveys does not provide an indication of the quality or impact of survey programs. From an evaluation provided by survey practitioners within the high-tech industry, Kraut reported that the two most positive outcomes of organizational surveys are improving organizational functioning and improving communication. He also reported that the two greatest failings of survey programs are the lack of action taken on survey findings and that the survey instrument did not tap critical issues and concerns and was therefore of questionable value. In this book, I directly address both of these common failings.

> As Kraut (2006) noted, the popularity of surveys does not provide an indication of the quality or impact of survey programs.

The Thesis of This Book

Clearly the majority of large organizations today are using employee survey methodology in an effort to improve the way they manage their talent and drive their overall business success. Leadership and management teams in industrialized countries worldwide are using the method. In addition, the use of employee surveying is increasing and will likely continue to increase over the next generation, in line with the fifteen-year trend established in the United States.

The thesis of this book is that in order to maximize the effectiveness of the employee survey method, the survey program itself must be strategic, and must be seen in this way. Something is strategic when it is important to the completion of a strategic plan or of great importance to an integrated or planned effort. In other words, the survey program should fit into a larger whole of the business strategy.

My contention is that many organizations do an employee survey simply because they think it is a good thing to do, that others (read: competitors) are doing it, and that it shows interest in the morale and welfare of their workforce. Indeed, surveys are a good thing to do, many organizations are doing them, and the doing of them typically shows interest in the morale and welfare of employees. My point is that survey programs will produce the greatest return on investment when they are consciously used as part of the organization's business strategy. Why is this so important? It is of utmost importance because it is from a strategic starting point that the best decisions will be made about what to measure, when to measure it, and how to use that measurement for the greatest gain.

Survey programs will produce the greatest return on investment when they are consciously used as part of the organization's business strategy.

The Strategic Survey Model

From over thirty years in the practice of employee surveys, I conclude that organizations generally conduct surveys for four, sometimes overlapping, reasons. These reasons exist along a continuum of "defensive" to "offensive" reasons. Starting with the most defensive reason and as originally stated in an earlier book (Wiley, 2006), the four reasons are:

1. To identify warning signs of trouble within the organization
2. To evaluate the effectiveness of specific programs, policies, and initiatives
3. To gauge the organization's status or strength as an employer of choice among its workforce
4. To predict and drive organizational outcomes, including customer satisfaction and business performance

A major implication of the model (see Figure 1.1) is that achieving the specific purpose requires survey content designed for or tailored to each strategic objective. The employee survey questions

Figure 1.1 Strategic Survey Model

Copyright © Kenexa 2010.

that best predict customer satisfaction and loyalty, for example, are very different from those that best predict where employees will be most susceptible to union organizing attempts.

Major Objectives for Employee Surveying

In the remainder of the chapter, I introduce each major objective for employee surveying. I also elaborate on the primary purpose of the book and the flow that supports that purpose.

Employee Surveys as Warning Indicators

An employee survey can serve as an early-warning indicator of a problem or potential problem in an organization. This is the most defensive reason for conducting an employee survey. In this sense, it is a red flag, indicating danger ahead. An organization may decide to conduct a survey of this type for several reasons.

One reason could be a belief in the fundamental importance of creating and sustaining an ethical work environment. Given some of the highly visible and costly ethical lapses of the past decade, many organizations have given extra attention to ethics in the workplace based on the belief that an ethical work environment is not only the right thing to do but is also associated in the long run with superior business performance (Kotter and Heskett, 1992). Thus, measuring the perceived support for ethics and the extent to which employees view coworkers and managers as behaving in an ethical manner are natural extensions of the strategic emphasis the organization is placing on ethics. When survey results indicate an ethical lapse or a perceived decline over time in the support for ethics in the organization, the survey is proving its value as an early-warning indicator, and its leaders can take the appropriate steps to address the issues raised before they become more serious. Employee surveys as warning indicators are the focus of Chapter Two.

Employee Surveys as Program Evaluation Measures

An employee survey can serve as a program evaluation measure by assessing the effectiveness of a major corporate policy, program, or initiative. This may occur after implementing the program fully, or the assessment could take place before or during the implementation of a program and therefore influence the program's final design. Either way, the concept is to use employee input to evaluate the effectiveness of a policy, program, or initiative in order to make decisions about needed adjustments. An organization may decide to conduct this type of survey for several reasons.

For example, many organizations have determined they need strong policies and practice implementation to support the goal of creating a more diverse workforce. A current shortage of talent, more intense global competition, and the need to pursue new international markets are the types of economic trends that place a priority on the ability of organizations to do a better job of recruiting and retaining women and minority group members. In this view, creating a more diverse workforce becomes a strategic imperative in the management of the organization's talent. As a result, leadership needs to know, for example, the extent to which employees believe that management is committed to diversity, how easy it is for people from diverse backgrounds to fit into the organization and be accepted, and whether the organization enables people from diverse backgrounds to excel. A well-designed survey and an appropriately analyzed set of survey results provide that type of evaluation. Employee surveys as program evaluation measures are the focus of Chapter Three.

Employee Surveys as Measures of Employer of Choice

An employee survey can serve as a measure of employer of choice. The questions on this type of survey typically measure (1) the key factors that cause or help explain why employees choose to stay with their current employer, (2) the level of employee engagement, and (3) the major drivers of employee engagement.

The employer-of-choice terminology came into popular use in the 1990s as a way of capturing the importance of the employer's being attractive to both current and prospective employees as a place to work. The notion is tied, of course, to the idea of the war for talent, colorful language used to acknowledge the competition for labor, particularly knowledge workers. This talent pool is especially critical to whether an organization can implement its business strategy. Thus, for some organizations, being an employer of choice is a business imperative and a necessary element of their business strategy. In my estimation, this is the most commonly conducted type of survey in organizations today. Employee surveys as measures of employer of choice are the focus of Chapter Four.

Employee Surveys as Leading Indicators of Business Success

An employee survey can serve as a leading indicator of business success. This is the most "offensive" reason for conducting a survey and is becoming, in the more globalized and competitive marketplace, an increasingly common reason that organizations choose to implement the employee survey methodology.

Using an employee survey as a leading indicator of business success is tied to linkage research (Wiley, 1996), which explores the relationship between how employees describe their work environment and other critical success measures, such as customer satisfaction and business performance. Dozens of studies have been published that demonstrate that more favorable descriptions of the work environment (as measured by employee surveys) are significantly correlated with customer satisfaction ratings as well as an array of business performance measures. Many of these studies, conducted in the service industry, reveal that employee survey topics such as customer orientation, quality emphasis, involvement, and training (Wiley, 1996) are particularly effective in predicting customer satisfaction, loyalty, and repeat business. Thus, if an element of an organization's business strategy is to distinguish itself based on customer service, it may use an employee survey containing the previously listed topics (for example, customer orientation) to serve as a leading indicator of actual customer satisfaction and behavior. Employee surveys as leading indicators of business success are the focus of Chapter Five.

Purpose and Flow of This Book

I believe the purpose of an employee survey program is to support the organization's business strategy. I also believe an employee survey does this primarily in two ways: providing actionable information about the business strategy and a sensible approach and process for the use of the resulting data. The purpose of this book is to help those working internal to organizations make the best decisions possible when designing their overall survey program. In other words, it is to help internal executive sponsors and practitioners to think through very clearly their purpose in surveying so that their program design decisions will flow naturally and will align with the program's overarching goals. This book is not about the logistics of surveying, such as how to administer a survey and design survey reports. Instead, I focus on what I believe to be higher-order issues: survey purpose, survey content, and the discussion and use of survey results to make lasting and positive impacts on the organization.

Chapters Two through Five highlight the primary uses of employee surveys: as warning indicators, program evaluation measures, measures of employer of choice, and leading indicators of business success. Chapter Six reviews a hybrid survey—one that combines the employer-of-choice and leading-indicators-of-business-success purposes. This review unfolds as part of a larger discussion introducing a new High Performance–Engagement Model. These topics form Part One of the book.

Part Two focuses on the effective use of survey results to affect change in the organization. Chapter Seven discusses action planning and looks at successful techniques. Chapter Eight acknowledges the increased use of survey results in strategic goal setting and provides suggestions on how best to do this. Chapter Nine reviews what I believe are requirements for sustaining positive change in survey results over time. Chapter Ten summarizes these messages and provides a few concluding thoughts.

Chapter Two

Employee Surveys as Warning Indicators

The most "defensive" use of an employee survey is as an early-warning indicator, or red flag, for a problem or potential problem within the organization. Higgs and Ashworth (1996) discuss this use of employee surveys dating back to the 1930s and 1940s. During that period, especially in the United States, employee surveys were used to identify worker groups with low morale that might be susceptible to union organizing attempts. With the identification of alienated groups, organizations could convert their survey results into actions aimed at addressing concerns and grievances, thus reducing the possibility that employees would turn to third-party representation (unions) for redress of their issues and complaints.

For an employee survey to be a warning indicator, its content must produce results indicating the extent to which a serious problem lies ahead. In this way, survey results serve to inform management that action is needed in order to prevent a problem from becoming more serious and more detrimental to achieving organizational objectives.

The starting point for this type of survey can be specific management concerns: complaints, accidents, reports of unethical or illegal behavior, or other evidence suggesting a problem. The starting point may also be a more proactive management stance, that is, taking the initiative to prevent problems from occurring. Regardless of starting point, a survey of this type may be undertaken to cover a wide range of organizational issues. This chapter offers three such examples: using the survey as a warning indicator of safety problems, ethical lapses, and vulnerability to unionization.

Safety Issues: The Employee Survey as a Warning Indicator

Concerns about safety may range from physical harm to employees as a result of unsafe working conditions, to workplace violence or substance abuse, to security of organizational and personal property (Wiley, 2006). Perhaps most often, a survey may be used to identify gaps among the organization's policies, procedures, and objectives with regard to safety and the reality of those safety issues, as perceived by employees.

Specifically, typical objectives of safety surveys are to:

- Use employees as observers of safety practices
- Measure the level of importance employees place on safety
- Evaluate the need to make employees more conscious of safety
- Determine whether employees are willing to report safety violations
- Determine whether employees receive a satisfactory response when they report on unsafe behaviors of their coworkers or other safety issues

A safety-related survey may include topics such as these:

- Management sets an example for safety.
- Safety is valued over budget or schedule.
- Management responds appropriately to the reporting of safety issues.
- Safety procedures are clear and understood.
- Everyone is protected from health or safety hazards.
- Sufficient nearby medical facilities are available.
- The organization is a leader regarding employee safety.

For specific industries and job types, the issue of safety takes on a higher level of importance. For organizations in some industries, their emphasis on and reputation regarding safety will influence their ability to recruit employees, as well as their corporate citizenship record in the marketplace and community. Thus, the measurement of safety through an employee survey and the use of safety survey results to affect organizational change is an important part of leaders' overall organization strategy and certainly an important part of their human capital strategy.

For specific industries and job types, the issue of safety takes on a higher level of importance.

Entire surveys can be devoted to the measurement of safety. When an organization makes a decision to design and administer a safety survey, it will likely measure the types of issues previously listed. Although it is not uncommon to devote an entire survey to a single topic, much more common is the practice of including a module or dimension of safety-related items in a longer multitopic survey. A dimension is a specific combination of items that measures the same psychological construct. In the example presented in Table 2.1, the dimension is labeled "Health and Safety," and the specific item wording is:

- Safety is a priority in my organization.
- People in my work area are protected from health and safety hazards.
- How do you rate the safety of your overall working conditions?
- How do you rate your overall work environment (ventilation, noise, lighting, space, and so forth)?

Table 2.1 presents both the dimension score and item-level results for the health and safety dimension. These results are based on the 2009 WorkTrends survey and presented in percentage favorable, the most common method of reporting survey results (and computed as the percentage of respondents who selected one of the two most favorable options on a 5-point Likert rating scale).

Table 2.1 Global Scores on the Health and Safety Dimension

Health and Safety	Percentage Favorable
Dimension score	60
Items	—
1. Safety is a priority.	60
2. People in my work area are protected.	63
3. Safety of working conditions.	64
4. Rating of physical work environment.	54

According to Table 2.1, 60 percent of the global workforce rates health and safety issues favorably. Among the four items, the overall rating of the safety of working conditions achieves the most favorable response. In fact, its rating of 64 percent favorable exceeds the favorable rating of the physical work environment by ten percentage points. These global averages are only a starting point in the interpretation and use of these types of results.

As noted earlier, concerns about employee health and safety are of considerably greater importance to some industries. Figure 2.1 provides an international ranking of key industries on the dimension of health and safety. The industries scoring most favorably are mining, banking and financial services, high-tech manufacturing, and construction and engineering. The industries scoring least favorably are personal services and agriculture, farming, and forestry. That the scores for the mining and construction industries are among the highest is no doubt testimony to the safety practices put into place by management for workers operating in physically difficult and potentially dangerous circumstances. In fact, on the single item "Where I work, safety is a priority," the industry achieving the most favorable score is mining (77 percent favorable). For those working in farming, agriculture, and forestry, where workers also face physically difficult and potentially dangerous circumstances, management support appears much weaker (51 percent favorable).

Figure 2.1 Global Industry Ranking on the Health and Safety Dimension

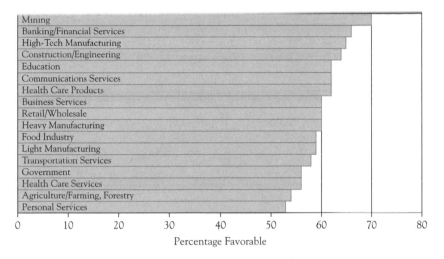

Percentage Favorable

Figure 2.2 shows the differences in major job types in ratings of their employer's stance on health and safety issues. These results, also from the WorkTrends study, indicate vast differences by job type. The scores for managers and senior managers and executives outpace the scores for laborers, operatives, and those in the skilled trades by approximately fifteen percentage points. In fact, less than half of the latter group rates the dimension favorably. Part of this gap no doubt is due to differences in the quality of the physical working conditions in which these two employee segments operate. However, these results also reveal clear differences between these two worker segments in their perceptions of health and safety in the workplace. This type of gap in organization-level survey results is a red flag indicating the need to understand why frontline workers rate the health and safety issues the way they do and why their opinions differ so much from those of managers and senior managers and executives.

A safety survey is administered to help an organization evaluate its climate for safety. This may lead to a determination that additional training for employees or management is warranted. It may also identify safety concerns or issues that were previously

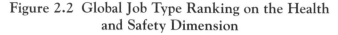

Figure 2.2 Global Job Type Ranking on the Health
and Safety Dimension

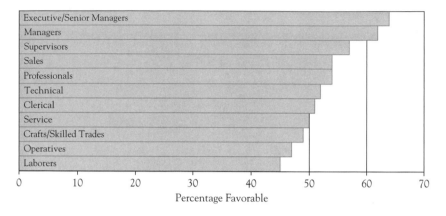

unknown to management. One of the most important functions of a safety-based employee survey is to disabuse management of the belief that simply because a safety policy is in place, they have successfully addressed safety issues throughout the organization. Safety surveys and other surveys that serve as warning indicators reveal how successfully policies and procedures are implemented at the workforce level.

Ethical Issues: The Employee Survey as a Warning Indicator

The topics of corporate ethics, integrity and honesty in business conduct, and operating according to legal standards have attracted considerable attention over the past decade. Many organizations have been embarrassed and have seen their corporate reputations suffer because of revelations of fraud, scandal, and illegal behavior. Some organizations, such as Enron and WorldCom, have been destroyed and their past leaders imprisoned because of illegal and unethical conduct.

The challenges of maintaining an ethical work environment are broad. Leaders and employees in virtually all organizations, regardless of size, may be challenged with maintaining the law and upholding high standards of ethics and integrity in business conduct.

The challenges of maintaining an ethical work environment are broad.

Increasingly organizations are relying on employee survey results to determine the extent to which the articulated values and ethical standards established by senior management are being disseminated and propagated throughout the organization's culture. This makes sense because surveys provide employees a confidential and typically anonymous means of communicating concerns over ethical lapses and observations regarding dishonesty, fraud, and other inappropriate behaviors. In this respect, an ethics and integrity survey can serve as a warning indicator of an ethics problem.

Similar to the topic of safety, ethics and integrity can be measured through a single topic survey or through a module of items contained within a longer multitopic survey. I have implemented programs using both such approaches. In fact, working in partnership with the Center for Ethical Business Cultures, we designed a standard twenty-seven-item survey addressing ethics and integrity. These items, and the dimensions under which they are subsumed, reflect the framework the center has developed for building ethical work environments.

The essence of the ethics and integrity survey is captured in the Integrity QuickCheck, a five-item index measuring senior management behavior, coworker behavior, and organizational values and practices:

- Ethical issues and concerns can be discussed without negative consequences.

- Senior management supports and practices high standards of ethical behavior.

- My organization strives to serve the interests of multiple stakeholders (for example, customers, employees, suppliers, and community), not just the shareholders.

- The behavior of the people I work with is consistent with our mission, vision, and values.

- People do not get ahead unless their behavior clearly demonstrates the organization's values.

Table 2.2 presents the overall Integrity QuickCheck score as well as the scores for the individual index items. These results are drawn from the WorkTrends survey. In general, these results are disappointing, if not actually alarming, given that the worldwide average for the Integrity QuickCheck index score stands at only 54 percent favorable. Among the results for the five individual items, employees indicate slightly more support for the organization's serving the interests of multiple stakeholders (57 percent favorable) and slightly less support for people needing to behave in a way consistent with organizational values in order to get ahead (50 percent favorable). The scores for the other items fall in between these two scores.

The results for the Integrity QuickCheck by country are presented in Figure 2.3. From this ranking, the differences by country range almost thirty percentage points between the highest- and lowest-rated countries. Clearly those working in India, Canada, the United States, and Brazil rate support for

Table 2.2 Global Scores on the Integrity QuickCheck Index

Integrity QuickCheck Index	Percentage Favorable
Dimension score	54
Items	—
1. Ethical issues can be openly discussed.	54
2. Senior management behaves ethically.	56
3. The organization serves multiple stakeholders.	57
4. Coworkers act consistently with values.	53
5. People do not get ahead unless their behavior demonstrates organizational values.	50

Figure 2.3 Country Ranking on the Integrity QuickCheck Index Score

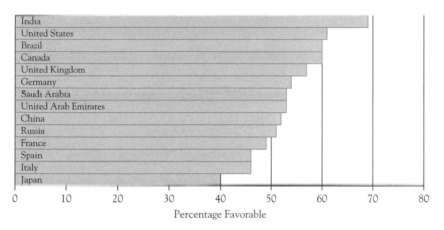

Percentage Favorable

ethics and ntegrity the highest. However, fewer than half of the workers in the western European countries of France, Spain, and Italy observe strong support for ethics and integrity. If nothing else, this figure displays how entities (in this case, countries) can differ significantly on this important leadership topic.

Building an organizational culture that operates according to established and communicated values requires ongoing attention and effort on the part of senior leadership—an investment that has bottom-line ramifications. For example, a series of studies by Kotter and Heskett (1992) found that organizations with cultures focused on balancing the interests of multiple stakeholders (customers, employees, and investors) and ensuring proper management skills at all leadership levels outperformed those with a disproportionate focus on short-term financial gains. Over the eleven-year time frame studied, organizations with a balanced focus increased revenues by an average of 682 percent, while those more narrowly focused on short-term financial gains increased revenues by only 166 percent. Other business results, including net income, stock price, and employee head count levels, also increased at significantly higher margins in organizations with more balanced cultures.

The WorkTrends findings presented below reinforce the conclusion that the extent of support employees perceive for ethics and integrity is related to performance outcomes. For this analysis, two subgroups of employees were created from the WorkTrends database: those who experience strong support for integrity in the workplace and those who experience weak support. Those in the strong-support segment could answer all five items comprising the Integrity QuickCheck index favorably. This represents 23 percent of all employees surveyed. Those in the weak-support segment responded either neutrally or unfavorably to all five items in the index. This represents 16 percent of all employees surveyed. We then computed the scores for each group on the following two questions: (1) How has your organization's reputation changed in the past year? and (2) How has your organization's performance changed in the past year? These questions could be answered on a five-point scale ranging from much better to much worse. The results in Figure 2.4 display the extent to which employees in the two groups indicate organization reputation and performance improvement over the past twelve months.

Figure 2.4 Strength of Ethical Culture and Reputation and Performance Improvement

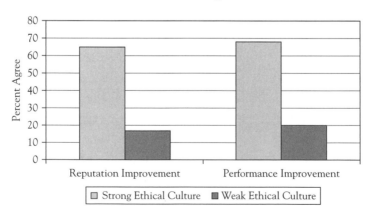

These conclusions make a clear case for establishing strong ethical work environments. Those who work in a strong ethical culture are three to four times more likely to say that their organization's reputation and performance have improved over the previous twelve months in comparison to those who work in a weak ethical culture. These results reinforce Kotter and Heskett's findings that leadership practices that help create and sustain a strong ethical work environment also produce superior business results.

There are other reasons, beyond serving as a warning indicator, that surveying employees on ethics and integrity may prove valuable. For example, if an organization has determined it is necessary to acquire other organizations in order to achieve its strategic purposes, it may choose to survey the newly acquired organization to assess the values that are dominant within the existing cultures and then assess its progress in establishing a new standard.

Obviously the results of surveys related to ethics and integrity can help organizational leaders develop a plan of action, including targeted education and training programs for managers and employees, improved corporate communications, compliance audits, advancement and recognition programs, changes in hiring standards and performance reviews, and other specific tools. The actions trace their history back to a well-designed employee survey crafted to assess the extent to which a problem or potential problem exists within an organization.

Union Vulnerability: The Employee Survey as a Warning Indicator

This final example represents one of the most appealing applications of employee survey technology as a red flag or warning indicator. As Higgs and Ashworth note, this use of employee surveys dates all the way back to nonunionization efforts in the 1930s. For obvious strategic and financial reasons, most businesses in North America continue to resist unionizing programs. In their view, unions can serve as an impediment to workforce communications by inserting a third party between workers and managers, thereby reducing the effectiveness of an organization's implementation and alignment of corporate strategy.

In many geopolitical regions around the world, the drive for unionization is typically based on worker dissatisfaction over issues such as pay, benefits, job security, and working conditions. Inherent in such worker disgruntlement are two underlying concerns: the perception of a lack of fair treatment and lack of respect. When properly designed, employee surveys can be important tools in identifying locations, worker groups, work shifts, specific management practices, and issues that stoke a desire for third-party representation. Informed by the results of employee surveys, organizational leadership can take corrective steps to defuse the underlying worker concerns that often create the opening to union organizing campaigns.

Informed by the results of employee surveys, organizational leadership can take corrective steps to defuse the underlying worker concerns that often create the opening to union organizing campaigns.

In the late 1970s, along with other industrial-organizational psychologists, I was a member of the personnel research function at Ford Motor Company. One of our responsibilities was the oversight of the salaried employee satisfaction survey program. A purpose of the survey program was to use the results to identify groups of salaried employees who might find the arguments for unionization appealing. Indeed, at that time among labor relations experts in the automotive and other heavy manufacturing industries, the unionization of segments of the white-collared salaried workforce was a palpable concern. This concern led to the inclusion in Ford's survey of a union vulnerability index (UVI). The design of the index was based on common knowledge of the precursors to unionization, what was gleaned from other researchers also interested in assessing worker vulnerability to unionization, and Ford's own research. Since that time, I have used this index in surveys designed for organizations wanting to understand the extent to which their workers might be susceptible to the arguments of third-party representation.

The UVI is a set of nine items that efficiently summarizes employee opinions on a range of critical employee relations issues:

- Pay
- Benefits
- Job security
- Working conditions
- Fair treatment
- Recognition
- Opportunity to get a better job
- Overall job satisfaction
- Overall organization satisfaction

Past research, much of it conducted by internal corporate research functions and thus not available in the public domain, indicates the UVI is a useful predictor of worker discontent and relative vulnerability to unionization.

The UVI is calculated as the composite score of the nine items listed and is reported as percentage unfavorable (the percentage of respondents who selected one of the two most unfavorable options on a 5-point Likert rating scale). The focus on percentage unfavorable is logical since the UVI is a measure of worker discontent. Typically survey results would be evaluated to identify those units within the organization whose UVI scores placed them at more risk or higher in the range of moderate risk.

Rules of Interpretation for the Union Vulnerability Index

A score:

- Less than or equal to 15 percent unfavorable identifies organizational units of less risk.
- Between 16 and 29 percent unfavorable identifies organizational units of moderate risk.
- Thirty percent or more unfavorable identifies organizational units of more risk.

To place these rules of interpretation into context, consider Figure 2.5, which presents a ranking of U.S. industries based on their UVI scores. It is especially important to note that these data are drawn from workers who are not currently represented by a union. The heavy manufacturing, restaurant, communication services, and retail and hotel industries have the highest UVI scores: they fall in the middle of the moderate-risk category. The industries with the lowest UVI scores are accounting/legal,

Figure 2.5 Union Vulnerability for Selected U.S. Industries

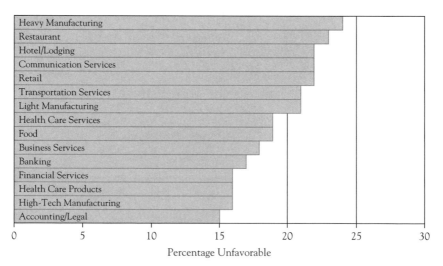

financial services, health care products, and high-tech manufacturing. The score for the accounting/legal industry places it in the category of less risk, and the scores for the other industries are at the very low end of the moderate-risk category. Of course, these are industry averages, meaning that the scores of individual organizations may vary significantly from this norm.

Figure 2.6 displays the ranking of the UVI scores for major U.S. job types. Again, it is important to highlight that these data are drawn from workers who are not currently represented by a union. Perhaps not surprising, the job types with the highest UVI scores are laborers (production workers, assemblers, packers, and so on), operatives (equipment operators, drivers, deliverers, and others), and service workers. Scores for these job types place them in the middle to upper end of the moderate-risk category. Those with the lowest UVI scores are executives (below even the "less risk" threshold) and those in technical/professional and managerial roles, whose scores fall at the very low end of the moderate-risk category. Once again, these are national averages, covering the entire swath of the U.S. workforce. Job type scores vary significantly by specific organizational conditions.

Figures 2.5 and 2.6 provide a glimpse of how those in different circumstances characterize their work environments along the continuum of union vulnerability. How is the UVI applied in practice? Let's consider an example.

Figure 2.6 Union Vulnerability by U.S. Worker Job Type

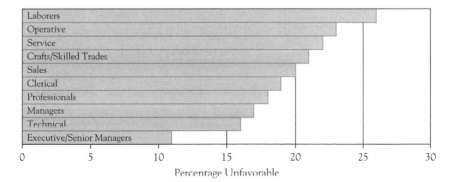

A survey was conducted for a large retailer in Canada that had recently acquired a new chain of stores in which employee activities related to unionization had been observed. Union avoidance was an important factor in this organization's labor relations and its overall business strategies. The survey we designed covered a number of topics and included the nine-item UVI. The idea was to use the UVI results to identify units—in this case, retail outlets—with the highest susceptibility to union organizing campaigns. Interpretive guidelines were used to rank the retailer's ninety outlets; three stores were categorized as "more risk" and eighteen stores as "moderate risk." Following the presentation of survey results, the client mentioned that known union activity had occurred in all three stores in the more-risk category, as well as one of the higher-scoring locations within the moderate-risk category. Based on the UVI results, leadership sent corporate employee relations teams to each of these locations and several of the other higher-scoring moderate-risk locations to investigate the sources of employee concerns and disgruntlement. Its overall follow-up strategy and the corrective actions taken proved successful. All of the stores within this retail chain remain union free to this day.

This example provides support for the validity of the UVI as a predictor of union vulnerability. The UVI does not predict the outcome of a union election. What it does measure are those factors known to give rise to the interest in third-party representation: dissatisfaction with pay, benefits, job security, and working conditions. To provide further validation of the UVI, the results in Table 2.3, derived from WorkTrends, present unique findings from U.S. workers currently working in a union-free environment. As part of the survey, they were asked: "If you had the chance, would you vote in favor of unionizing your organization?" UVI scores are presented for both those who would favor a union and those who would not.

The differences in scores between these two groups are staggering. The average UVI score for those who would vote pro-union

Table 2.3 UVI Scores for Pro-Union and Anti-Union U.S. Workers

	Percentage Unfavorable		Percentage Point Difference
	Pro-Union	Anti-Union	
UVI score	32	14	18
Items			
Satisfaction with recognition	47	23	24
Opportunity for a better job	44	23	21
Overall satisfaction with organization	35	14	20
Satisfaction with pay	33	14	20
Satisfaction with job	30	13	17
Satisfaction with job security	26	11	15
Satisfaction with benefits	25	10	15
Manager treats employees fairly	28	13	15
Overall physical work environment	19	7	11
Other items most distinguishing the two groups			
Seriously considering leaving organization	36	63	27
Opportunity for career development	43	22	21
Promising future at organization	38	18	21
Reasonable stress level	40	21	19
Management concern for employee well-being	40	20	19
Gladly refer friend or family member	32	13	19
Confidence in senior leaders	38	19	19
Senior management demonstrates employee importance	36	17	19
Ethical issues openly discussed	30	12	18
Communication is open and two way	39	21	18
Management makes use of employee ideas	34	16	17

is eighteen percentage points higher than for those who are anti-union. Interestingly, the UVI score for pro-union workers places them in the more-risk category, while the respective score for the anti-union workers shows them at the cusp of the less-risk category. The differences on the UVI items between these two groups of employees are among the highest of all item-level differences. Other items showing large differences between the two groups are also displayed in Table 2.3, providing further insight into the conditions that help create organizational vulnerability for unionization.

This analysis demonstrates that a full-fledged survey designed to serve as a warning indicator of union vulnerability should also contain these topics:

- Leadership: Generating confidence among and communicating the importance of employees
- Managers: Showing concern for employees and using employee ideas
- Growth and development: Having a promising future, with an opportunity for career development
- Communication: Open, including discussions of ethical concerns
- Job and organization: Reasonable stress levels, intent to stay, willingness to recommend

Such a survey would measure not only those topics long understood to underlie worker interest in third-party representation (the topics covered by the UVI) but topics measuring the orientation of leaders, the behavior of managers, opportunities for growth and development, openness of communication, and a few additional topics covering the job and the overall organization. Of course, the results of such a survey create only the foundation for effective survey follow-up and action planning. It remains the responsibility of organizational leadership to address issues of fairness, respect, and concern for workers, thus reducing worker interest in the typical arguments brought forward in union organizing campaigns.

Summary

One of the key premises of this book is that employee surveys should be designed to support organizational strategy. This chapter provides examples of how employee surveys can detect problems or potential problems within the organization or its workforce with regard to safety, ethics, and union vulnerability. When such problems are identified, management can take corrective actions aimed at bolstering the organization's strategy. The value of an employee survey program is maximized as the survey initiative in general, and survey content in particular, is consciously designed to support the strategic imperative.

Chapter Three

Employee Surveys as Program Evaluation Measures

In addition to serving as a warning indicator, an employee survey can be used to evaluate the effectiveness of an organizational policy, program, or initiative. The idea is to use the survey results gathered from the program evaluation to guide program design, whether it is final design or redesign. Either way, employee input plays a critical role in influencing how initiatives are implemented and policies are applied.

Employee benefit packages provide an example. Organizations often survey employees to evaluate the attractiveness of alternative benefit programs and elements, and then they develop or modify the final package based on employee feedback. As in the earlier discussion of surveys as warning indicators, organizations may devote an entire survey to a single topic they want assessed from the employee perspective, or they may incorporate one or more program evaluation types of measures into a longer multi-topic survey.

In this chapter, I provide two examples. The first illustrates using employee surveys to measure the effectiveness of diversity programs. The second focuses on evaluating another increasingly common organizational policy initiative: work/life balance.

The Employee Survey as a Program Evaluation Measure: Diversity

Economic trends such as shortage of talent, global competition, and the pursuit of new international markets cause organizations to place a priority on increasing their effectiveness in recruiting and retaining women and members of minority groups. This is an area where proper gathering and segmentation of employee survey data can help organizations identify key workplace factors that influence retention among specific subsets of the employee population.

Table 3.1 shows the results of a survey conducted at a major U.S. banking organization. These results demonstrate that relying on overall survey results to measure the success of an important policy initiative such as diversity can be entirely misleading

Relying on overall survey results to measure the success of an important policy initiative such as diversity can be entirely misleading.

and that significant differences generally exist in the responses among employees in different racial and ethnic origin groups. For example, in 2007, while scores for this organization's

Table 3.1 Banking Industry Case Study: Diversity Scores by Racial and Ethnic Origin Group

Overall and Major Ethnic Origin Group Scores (in Percentage Favorable)					
	Overall	*Asian*	*African American*	*Hispanic*	*White*
Dimension score	72	70	54	72	75
Items	—	—	—	—	—
1. Organization makes it easy for diverse backgrounds to fit in	79	78	65	80	81
2. Opinions valued regardless of background	73	71	55	73	76
3. Managers hire and retain diverse workforce	64	65	49	66	68
4. Employees developed and advanced regardless of background	70	65	47	69	73
Percentage of respondents	100	6	14	8	68

diversity dimension overall show an overall favorable response of 72 percent, segmentation by race reveals only 54 percent of African Americans responded favorably.

This banking organization has conducted four employee surveys since 1996 in which the measurement of progress on its diversity initiative has played a prominent role. Because of the segmentation analysis, organizational leadership has been able to target actions to improve these results and hold managers accountable for progress. Between 2000 and 2004 (see Table 3.2), the bank's communications and actions to support diversity were highly visible and focused on the training of employees and management, publicizing progress against goals, and placing diverse staff in higher-level and more visible positions. In 2004 expectations were high that the diversity dimension scores would continue to climb, but survey scores were lower than expected. Leadership concluded that not enough was being done to hire and promote minorities and that more emphasis on achieving diversity at senior levels was necessary. Since then, the bank has increased the number of high-level placements involving senior staff. The 2007 results reflect that emphasis, showing that the actions taken are proving successful.

This example illustrates the option of measuring progress on an important corporate initiative by including a content-specific

Table 3.2 Banking Industry Case Study: Diversity Dimension Trend Scores by Racial and Ethnic Origin Group (in Percentage Favorable)

Year	Overall	Asian	African American	Hispanic	White
1996	52	57	32	49	61
2000	66	59	47	60	73
2004	63	61	42	62	69
2007	72	70	54	72	75

dimension within a longer multitopic survey. Entire surveys devoted to a single topic represent the other primary option. This is what happened with another of my banking industry clients, also headquartered in the United States. In this instance, our team worked with the client's corporate diversity council to design and implement the survey program. The objectives of the survey were to:

- Provide the council with direction on how to improve the work environment for the support of diversity
- Satisfy the information needs of various segments of the organization's diverse employee population
- Support the multistep corporate diversity plan
- Send a strong message to the workforce regarding the value of diversity

A survey instrument was designed based on the client's diversity plan. The plan addressed these topics:

- Leaders' accountability for diversity
- People from diverse backgrounds in all levels of management
- Establishing long-term relationships with diverse communities
- Contributing to communities in which they work, live, and do business
- Ensuring diversity is present in all organization communications
- Being known as a diverse organization

For each step, four to six rating scale questions and one open-ended question were developed. In its final version, thirty-two rating scale questions were required to provide adequate coverage of the diversity plan. In addition, demographic questions were included in the survey to identify business unit, location, type of customer served, tenure, gender, manager/nonmanager status, racial and ethnic origin group, age, sexual orientation, and whether the respondent had a documented disability.

This case study is instructive for three reasons. First, for this corporation, workforce diversity is considered essential to achieving its business strategy. Thus, the survey was undertaken to measure progress against an important strategic initiative. Second, the survey was custom-designed against the explicit elements of its diversity strategy. This made it possible to identify plan elements that were being implemented successfully and those that required more attention. Third, the reporting of results was specific to various diverse elements of its workforce. Committees representing those diverse workforce segments could use the results to design new action plans supporting the overall objectives of the diversity plan. In addition, since this survey program was conducted over multiple years, the organization was able to track corporate progress. In fact, the second (and more recent) administration of the survey indicated progress of five percentage points in favorability as a grand average across the thirty-two rating scale questions. Progress on the six plan elements ranged from one to eight percentage points.

In my experience as a practitioner, it is more common to include the measurement of diversity within the context of a longer multitopic survey than to design a survey specifically to address this topic. In this approach, one or all of the following survey items are included in the diversity dimension:

- My organization has a strong track record for recruiting people from diverse backgrounds.
- My organization makes it easy for people from diverse backgrounds to fit in and be accepted.
- Diversity is very much a part of my organization's culture.

- The leadership at my organization is committed to diversity.
- My organization enables people from diverse backgrounds to excel.
- All employees, regardless of gender, ethnicity, religion, sexual orientation, and culture, have equal opportunities for advancement.

This set of items measures the overall culture for diversity and organizational leadership's commitment to diversity. It also covers many practices related to the support of diversity: recruitment, orientation, managerial support, and equal opportunities for advancement. These items can combine into a dimension score, as presented below.

Figure 3.1 results indicate that countries differ considerably in terms of how workers describe diversity support. In addition to workers in India, those in Canada, the United States, and Brazil rate their organizations most favorably on support for diversity. Interestingly, the United Arab Emirates, a country whose worker population is extremely mixed, reports a level of

Figure 3.1 Country Ranking on the Diversity Dimension

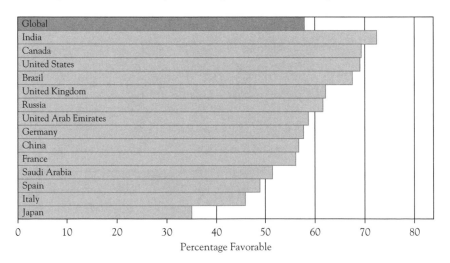

support for diversity that is roughly equal to the global average. And workers in another major Middle Eastern economic power, Saudi Arabia, report significantly less support for diversity. The lowest-ranking countries, where fewer than half of all workers describe favorably their organization's support for diversity, are Spain, Italy, and Japan.

Perhaps more interesting is the gender comparison provided in Table 3.3. Across the global study, women report more perceived support for diversity than men, though the margin of three percentage points, while significant in statistical terms, is insignificant in practical terms. Both men and women are most likely to report that their organizations have a strong track record for recruiting a diverse workforce and make it easy for those of a diverse background to fit in. Both men and women are least likely to feel that diversity is very much a part of their organization's culture. The largest difference between the two

Table 3.3 Global Gender Comparison on Diversity Dimension and Items

Diversity	Percentage Favorable	
	Male	Female
Dimension score	57	60
Items	—	—
1. Strong diversity recruiting record	61	63
2. Diversity backgrounds easily fit in	59	62
3. Equal advancement opportunities	58	63
4. Diverse organizational culture	56	58
5. Diverse enabled to excel	54	57
6. Leaders committed to diversity	52	55

gender groups taps into the belief that all employees, regardless of their background, have an equal opportunity to advance; 63 percent of women agree with that statement compared to only 58 percent of men.

Finally, and in my estimation most telling, Table 3.4 presents a special analysis of diversity at both the dimension and item score level by major racial and ethnic origin group. These results are produced from an analysis of a combined and equally weighted data set of two North American countries: Canada and the United States. As with the first client case study, this

Table 3.4 Racial and Ethnic Origin Group Diversity Comparison: Canada and the United States Combined

Diversity	Percentage Favorable				
	African Descent	American Indian	Asian Descent	Hispanic Descent	White
Dimension score	52	61	71	89	70
Items	—	—	—	—	—
1. Diverse organizational culture	58	59	70	94	69
2. Strong diversity recruiting record	56	68	74	94	72
3. Diverse backgrounds easily fit in	52	64	70	94	73
4. Diverse enabled to excel	49	55	69	94	67
5. Equal advancement opportunities	49	65	75	82	73
6. Leaders committed to diversity	47	52	65	79	63

more granular analysis uncovers startling differences among racial and ethnic origin groups. How employees of Hispanic descent describe organizational support for diversity differs quite significantly from employees of African descent. These results mirror what I typically find in client studies: those of Hispanic and Asian descent provide the most favorable ratings, and those of African descent and Native American Indians provide the least favorable ratings. Because the results for major racial ethnic groups can differ so dramatically, analyses such as those presented in Tables 3.3 and 3.4 should always be included in a review of organization-specific survey results on the topic of diversity.

> *How employees of Hispanic descent describe organizational support for diversity differs quite significantly from employees of African descent.*

The Employee Survey as a Program Evaluation Measure: Work/Life Balance

After several decades of growth in the proportion of women in the workforce, the concept of work/life balance emerged full force in the 1980s. As women increasingly were promoted into higher-level management positions, positions that made correspondingly greater demands on their time and energy, concerns about work/life balance became more urgent. Although concerns surrounding the balance of work and life responsibilities originated with women, men also began expressing a stronger desire for more balance in their lives, especially indicating the wish to be more involved in the lives and activities of their children. In addition, the demands of elder care were beginning to become more central for many middle-aged workers who increasingly were taking responsibility for the care of parents. Because of these and other life stresses and pressures, organizations began developing policies regarding work/life balance.

The need to develop organizational policies regarding work/life balance was clearly strategic: it was a matter of being able to attract and retain talent deemed essential to the organization's ability to meet its business objectives.

The need to develop organizational policies regarding work/life balance was clearly strategic.

Organizations began conducting work/life balance surveys in the late 1980s. Often these surveys were conducted organization-wide with an emphasis on analyzing results by gender. At that time, the clear expectation was that women would feel notably less support for work/life balance than men. While gender differences did emerge, especially early in the evolution of measuring work/life balance, the differences were almost never as great as expected, and they often showed the assessment (if not the actual experience) of work/life balance to be roughly similar for the two sexes.

Since most contemporary organizations understand the need for establishing a balance between work and life in order to develop the type of workforce necessary to achieve their business objectives, conducting entire surveys on the topic of work/life balance is less frequent than it was twenty years ago. More frequent is the practice of including a dimension assessing work/life balance in a longer multitopic survey. In such circumstances, I recommend a set of survey items that cover a range of related topics including the current work-related stress level, the extent to which one's life is currently well balanced, the degree of organizational support for work/life balance, and whether employees feel they must sacrifice career goals in order to balance work and life responsibilities. The following questions can be grouped together to create a work/life balance dimension:

- I can meet my career goals and still devote sufficient attention to my family and personal life.
- The stress level at work is reasonable.

- My life is well balanced among work, family and friends, and my personal needs.
- My organization supports employees' efforts to balance work and family and personal responsibilities.

The most common segmentation analysis on this topic is by gender. A global gender comparison is presented in Table 3.5. Consistent with what I find in the typical client-based study, this analysis reveals minimal differences between men and women. In fact, the overall work/life balance dimension score shows women are slightly more favorable in their general assessment. This finding has often puzzled management audiences who expected men to be much more favorable on this topic. Interestingly, the biggest difference at the item level shows men trailing women by four percentage points on the question about the extent to which one's employer supports employee efforts to balance work and family/personal responsibilities. Explanations for these results are often twofold: (1) women carry more of the load for meeting family and home responsibilities and thus are more sensitive to, familiar with, and favorable about ways in which organizations provide

Table 3.5 Global Gender Comparison on Work/Life Balance Dimension Items

Work/Life Balance	Percentage Favorable	
	Male	Female
Dimension score	54	55
Items	—	—
1. Can meet my career and personal goals	57	56
2. Life is well balanced	57	59
3. Stress level is reasonable	53	51
4. Organization supports work/life balance	48	52

support; and (2) higher-level positions, which often carry greater time demands, are still disproportionately occupied by men when compared to gender workforce composition statistics. In turn, the greater demands of the higher-level positions cause men to feel that their life is less well balanced and that their employer shows less support for helping them to achieve better work/life balance.

The second most common segmentation analysis of work/life balance survey results is by job type. Figure 3.2 provides a global ranking. This analysis reveals that (1) the most support for work/life balance is reported by senior and middle job managers (a finding that appears to negate one of the arguments previously presented); (2) managers are the only other job type notably above the global average; and (3) employees reporting the least support occupy the service, operative, and laborer job types. Satisfaction with work/life

Satisfaction with work/life balance appears to be directly correlated to amount of influence over how, and under what conditions, one performs one's work.

Figure 3.2 Global Job Types Ranking on the Work/Life Balance Dimension

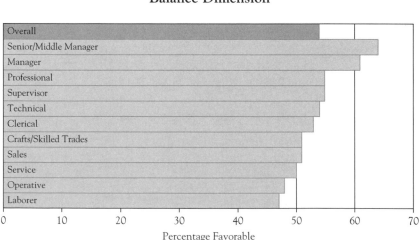

Percentage Favorable

balance appears to be directly correlated to amount of influence over how, and under what conditions, one performs one's work; the more influence, the higher the perceived support.

Summary

This chapter reviewed the concept of using an employee survey as an evaluative measure of a key organizational program, policy, or initiative. When relevant, employee opinions can be used to shape or redesign how a policy or a program is applied. Such employee input will contribute to the success of policy implementation and send a powerful message to employees about two things: what an organization considers important to its ability to meet its business objectives and that the organization wants and needs the input of employees to ensure the success of policy implementation. By way of example, an employee survey measuring an organization's benefits policies was briefly referenced; deeper illustrations of program evaluation measures were provided for the topics of diversity and work/life balance. The discussion of the latter two topics included specific examples of measurement technique as well as typical survey results.

Chapter Four

Employee Surveys to Measure Employer of Choice

The "employer-of-choice" terminology came into popular use in the 1990s as a way of capturing the importance of employers' being attractive to both prospective and current employees. Today recognition is bestowed on organizations that qualify as a great place to work. Annual listings published in high-visibility business magazines honor organizations for establishing and implementing progressive employee-oriented human resource policies that employees view favorably and often cite as reasons that they are reluctant to leave their current job to seek employment elsewhere. These annual lists garner significant attention among not only human resource professionals but CEOs and boards of directors as well. The employer-of-choice and great-place-to-work movements are natural extensions to the notion of the war for talent, which itself is dramatic and colorful language used to acknowledge the competition that exists for labor, particularly knowledge workers. This talent pool is often seen as critical to an organization's ability to implement its business strategy.

The desire to be known as an employer of choice also derives in part from a concern with a looming shortage of talent driven by Western culture demographics: baby boomer retirements and fewer younger workers entering the workforce. This serves to escalate the recruitment competition. Coupled with this is a focus on retention. Most organizations are acutely aware of the significant costs of turnover in terms of the recruitment, orientation, and training of new employees; short-term reduced productivity until new workers achieve an acceptable level of performance; and lost opportunities to realize a fuller return on investment when competent workers take their knowledge, skills, and abilities elsewhere (Wiley, 2006). Turnover cost estimates range from 25 to 200 percent of an employee's annual salary and benefits costs (TalentKeepers, 2005). Conventional wisdom places turnover costs at about 100 percent of the exiting employee's annual compensation.

The desire to be known as an employer of choice also derives in part from a concern with a looming shortage of talent.

At the time of this writing, the global economy is beginning to emerge from what has been labeled the Great Recession. As recovery strengthens and demand for products and services further rebounds, the emphasis on talent acquisition and talent retention will return. Perhaps more so than even before the recession, employees will be faced with making choices among employment options as to where and for whom they will work. When that occurs, employers will once again recognize that their corporate reputation and values impinge on their ability to compete in the war for talent. Attendant with that will be a renewed emphasis on employment branding as employers market their workforce culture, giving particular attention to their mission, vision, and values in the recruitment process (Wiley, 2006). Being an employer of choice will once again be a top business priority.

An employee survey can serve quite effectively as a measure of employer of choice and an indicator of how effectively the organization is fulfilling its employment brand promise. This type of survey typically contains questions that are known to measure the key factors that cause or help explain retention (that is, why employees choose to stay with their employer), the current level of employee engagement, and major drivers of employee engagement.

Employee Retention

Being an employer of choice is about being an organization where people are excited about coming to work, and once they are part of the team, they are excited about staying.

Fundamentally this speaks to employee engagement and retention. (Employee engagement is the broader topic and will be addressed later. This section focuses on what drives employee retention.) With that knowledge, the topics an employer-of-choice survey should include can be readily identified.

> *Being an employer of choice is about being an organization where people are excited about coming to work.*

Statistical analyses of survey results can help the employer understand the elements of the employment relationship that most influence a person's decision to stay or go. For example, it is common to include items in an employee survey such as, "I am seriously considering leaving within the next twelve months," or "I rarely think about looking for a new job with another organization." These types of items are treated as the dependent variable in a multiple regression or relative weights analysis. The other items in the survey are treated as independent variables and regressed against the measure of turnover intention or commitment to stay. The resultant analysis will identify items in the survey that most influence employee opinions about staying or leaving an organization.

Figure 4.1 shows the key drivers of retention for U.S. workers according to the 2009 WorkTrends survey. The following five elements of work most influence voluntary decisions to stay or leave:

1. Employee confidence in the organization's future success
2. Satisfaction with recognition received for a job well done
3. The employee's sense of the opportunities for future growth and development at the organization
4. A belief that the work itself matches well with one's skills and abilities
5. Organizational support for employees to achieve balance in work and life responsibilities

Figure 4.1 Key Drivers of 2009 U.S. Workforce Retention

Confidence in the future
Satisfied with recognition
Career development opportunity
Job matches skills/abilities
Work/life balance

Intent to Stay

Of course, Figure 4.1 is not a complete discussion of employee retention. Other factors are important as well. When consulting with clients, we discuss employee retention in the context of the push-friction-pull dynamic. The pull element refers to external opportunities another employer may provide: an opportunity for better compensation, faster advancement, better work/life balance, the appeal of working with an organization possessing a superior employment brand, or a combination of various factors. The friction is the interfering influence to a person's decision to leave. Those inhibitors to change include uncertainty, the value of existing relationships, family situations, and the potential of a trailing spouse who may need employment if the new job demanded relocation. The push element of the dynamic emerges from dissatisfaction with current employment that makes the employee more inclined to seek alternative employment and more susceptible to outside recruitment efforts.

An employer can do little to address the pull element of the retention dynamic. In the context of the war for talent, other employers will forever be searching for the talent they need to drive their business strategy. On the other hand, employers can control the push of employee dissatisfaction.

Just how important are these drivers in influencing intent to stay? Plotted in Figure 4.2 are stated turnover intention rates for two segments of the U.S. workforce: those who rate the retention drivers favorably and those who do not. If employees rate these aspects of their current employment favorably, their intent to stay averages forty-two percentage points higher. In other words, organizations that can provide employees with confidence, recognition,

Figure 4.2 Impact of Retention Drivers on Intent to Stay

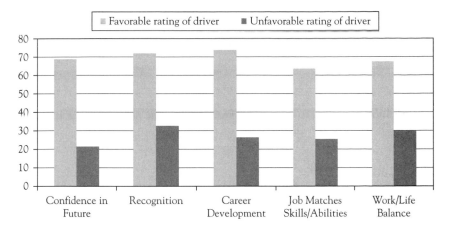

career development, a job matched well to their skills and abilities, and support for work/life balance will be dramatically more successful in their employee retention efforts.

Analyses of historical WorkTrends data show these influencers of retention have remained constant for the U.S. workforce over the past fifteen years. Figure 4.3 shows that, regardless of the exact year under consideration, four major factors emerge to influence employee decisions to stay or leave: confidence in the organization's future, feeling properly recognized for the contributions one makes, perceived opportunities for growth and development, and having a job well matched to one's skills and abilities.

Figure 4.3 Historical Drivers of Retention in the United States

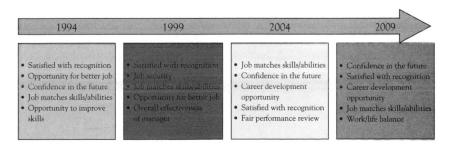

Generalizing about retention drivers within the U.S. workforce has merit because it helps us understand the underlying factors that cause workers to begin thinking about employment elsewhere. These analyses, and their historical reliability, provide guidance on what types of dimensions to include in a survey that has understanding employee voluntary turnover as one of its goals. Of course, the real benefit comes from taking corrective actions that prove successful in reducing unwanted turnover and its negative impact on business strategy implementation. However, in order to take such focused action, the organization needs to understand and properly measure the most potent drivers of turnover intent.

Exemplar items that validly and reliably measure these dimensions are shown in Table 4.1. Low scores on these retention drivers will direct managers and the organization at large toward solutions aimed at reducing future unwanted turnover.

Table 4.1 Items Related to Employee Decisions to Stay or Leave

Future/vision	I have confidence in the future of the organization.
	The organization is making the changes necessary to compete effectively.
Work itself	My job makes good use of my skills and abilities.
	I like the kind of work I do.
Growth and development	This organization provides me with the opportunity for growth and development.
	I feel there is a promising future for me in this organization.
Recognition	My manager provides me with recognition for doing good work.
	This organization values my contribution.

When these items are included in an organization's survey, the same analysis described earlier can be conducted. Retention drivers may differ for organizations in different countries and geographical regions, different industries, and even different stages of their evolution or organizational life cycle. Starting with informed general trends is only a first step; understanding how those trends play out in a situation provides superior guidance.

Segment analysis within an organization is also recommended because retention drivers may vary by job type or level. Executives and senior managers, professional and technical employees, and supervisors/managers (those often referred to as knowledge workers) may evaluate retention drivers differently from those who are in the laborer job category, for example. Table 4.2, which summarizes such an analysis, reveals a significant overlap of retention drivers for both types of worker. However, one of the top five drivers for those in the laborer category (production, assembly, packing, and material moving, for example) includes the quality of the physical work environment. And a unique driver for professional and technical employees is the opportunity to improve one's skills. Understanding these different drivers can help organizations tailor their retention practices accordingly.

Table 4.2 Retention Drivers by Job Type

Retention Drivers for Laborers	Retention Drivers for Professional/ Technical Employees
• Satisfied with recognition	• Confidence in the future
• Confidence in the future	• Career development opportunity
• Career development opportunity	• Satisfied with recognition
• Liking the work	• Job matches skills/abilities
• Quality of physical work environment	• Opportunity to improve skills

Employee Engagement

Employee engagement has been in the forefront of the discussion about employee motivation and commitment for the past ten years. Many organizations today have developed their survey programs around the measurement of employee engagement or have redirected the thrust of their program to provide a measure of employee engagement.

Many definitions of employee engagement have been developed and are accessible in the public domain. For the purposes of this discussion, the following definition will be used: employee engagement is the extent to which employees are motivated to contribute to organizational success and are willing to apply discretionary effort to accomplishing tasks important to the achievement of organizational goals. This definition implies that an engaged workforce will be motivated to perform, aligned toward organizational success, and willing to apply independent discretionary effort in order to achieve organizational goals. Thus, engagement is a state—a precursor to both a higher degree of commitment and intent to stay. In this sense, employee engagement is not performance, although it can influence the extent to which performance goals are met. Rather, employee engagement is a precondition that leads to greater performance. It will display itself in higher commitment to the achievement of organizational goals and a stronger intent to stay with one's employer. This view is captured in Figure 4.4.

Employee engagement is a precondition that leads to greater performance.

This figure implies that a more engaged employee is more conscientious about his or her work, more committed to achieving organizational goals, more productive, and less likely to be absent or to resign voluntarily. In aggregate, then, a more engaged workforce is a higher-performing workforce. In essence, employee engagement is a means to the end of helping the organization succeed.

Figure 4.4 Employee Engagement at the Employee Level

Engaged employees care more, perform better, stay longer

Employee engagement measurement must tie back to both its definition and the constructs that combine to create employee engagement. Kenexa has created such a measure in the form of the following 5-point Likert rating scale items:

1. I am proud to work for my organization.
2. Overall, I am extremely satisfied with my organization as a place to work.
3. I rarely think about looking for a new job with another organization.
4. I would gladly refer a good friend or family member to my organization for employment.

Combined, the equation produced from this operational definition is:

$$\text{Employee engagement} = \text{Pride} + \text{satisfaction} + \text{commitment} + \text{advocacy.}$$

If employee engagement is a state or condition, what influences it to be stronger or weaker? Developing a strategic employer-of-choice survey, in addition to including the employee engagement index, must also measure the topics or dimensions that drive it higher or lower. Measuring and then taking action on those dimensions will have a positive impact on employee engagement and ultimately influence commitment, motivation, and intent to stay.

The Drivers of Employee Engagement

The drivers of employee engagement may differ according to country, industry, job type, and other personal characteristics such as age generation group. One way to create a common framework for identifying the dimensions that most influence employee engagement is to develop a global database of the opinions of workers in countries representing the world's twelve largest economies, which account for 73 percent of the world's gross domestic product (see Chapter One).

Relative weights analysis is used to identify these global drivers of employee engagement:

1. Confidence in the organization's future
2. Organization supports work/life balance
3. Excited about one's work
4. Promising future for one's self
5. Safety is a priority
6. Corporate responsibility efforts increase overall satisfaction
7. Opportunity to improve one's skills
8. Satisfied with recognition
9. Confidence in the organization's senior leaders
10. Coworkers give their very best

These ten items are, on a global basis, those that most influence employee engagement index scores. In other words, the goal of increasing employee engagement can be achieved by improving the ratings on these ten drivers.

Drivers may differ by other important variables such as country, industry, or specific organization. Figure 4.5 reinforces that point.

There is no single country for which the global list is a perfect country-level match. However, for all countries, there is a match with at least seven of the global drivers.

Figure 4.5 Common Drivers of Employee Engagement

	Confidence in Organization's Future	Work/Life Balance	Excited About Work	Promising Future	Safety Is a Priority	Corporate Responsibility	Opportunity to Improve Skills	Recognition	Confidence in Senior Leaders	Coworkers Give Their Very Best
Brazil	●	●		●	●	●	●	●	●	●
Canada	●	●		●	●		●	●	●	
China	●	●		●	●		●			●
France	●	●	●	●	●		●	●		
Germany	●	●	●	●	●	●	●	●		
India	●	●	●	●	●	●	●	●	●	●
Italy	●	●	●	●	●	●	●	●		
Japan	●	●	●	●	●	●	●	●	●	
Russia	●	●	●	●	●	●	●	●	●	
Spain	●	●	●	●	●		●	●		
United Kingdom	●	●	●	●	●	●		●	●	●
United States	●	●	●	●	●	●	●	●	●	

Viewed more broadly, it seems reasonable to reduce this list of ten global drivers to summary statements. Employee engagement is really driven by four essential elements, or macrodrivers. In other words, employees are engaged by:

> *Employee engagement is really driven by four essential elements, or macrodrivers.*

- Leaders who inspire confidence in the future (drivers 1, 4, and 9)

- Managers who recognize employees and mobilize their teams for peak performance (drivers 8 and 10)

- Exciting work and the opportunity to improve their skills (drivers 3 and 7)

- Organizations that demonstrate a genuine responsibility to their employees and the communities in which they operate (drivers 2, 5, and 6)

This summary points us to the four basic sources of employee engagement: the behavior of leaders, the behavior of managers,

Figure 4.6 Prerequisites and Outcomes of Employee Engagement

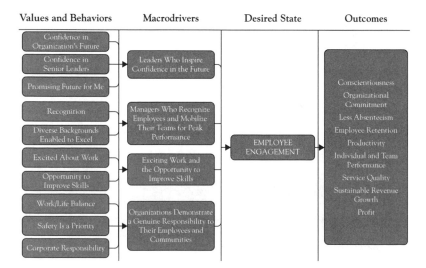

the work itself, opportunities it provides for skill enhancement, and the organization-level values and policies that stress care and concern for the employee and for the broader community. This allows us to build a model of employee engagement (see Figure 4.6) that reflects the required values and behaviors, summarized as macrodrivers, that produce the desired state of employee engagement. Also displayed in the figure are the consequences of having a more engaged workforce.

How Does Employee Engagement Relate to Business Success?

Kenexa has conducted studies for several of its clients showing that the units within those client organizations that have achieved higher employee engagement index scores have also achieved better scores on a number of outcome measures: absenteeism, productivity, sales, customer service, and profit. Some of these results are summarized in Table 4.3.

Implications for Survey Content

Returning to one of the main theses of this book, a strategic employee survey should fit and support an overarching business strategy. If the strategy is to be an employer of choice, that is, a place where people are excited about coming to work and once they arrive and are part of the team, they are excited about staying, what does that imply regarding survey content? An employer-of-choice survey aimed at measuring engagement and its drivers should include the types of items displayed in Table 4.4.

Of course, survey content should be tailored to the organization and its values. For example, some organizations may be well advanced in their corporate responsibility initiatives and see a need to measure progress regarding that topic; other organizations may just be starting down this path and feel that even getting a baseline measure is premature. Based on the research of the global

Table 4.3 Linking Employee Engagement to Business Results

Industry	Employee Engagement Predicts
Transportation/logistics	On-time delivery
Telecommunications	More favorable customer service ratings
	Likelihood of reaching the net income plan
Retail	Sales increase
	Net profit increase
Consumer products	Increase in productivity per hour
	Decrease in absenteeism
	Reduction in waste

Table 4.4 Macrodrivers and Exemplar Items

Macrodriver: Leaders who inspire confidence in the future
I have confidence in the future of this organization.
The leadership of this organization has communicated a vision of the future that motivates me.
I trust the leadership of this organization.
Leadership at this organization has the ability to deal with the challenges we face.
I feel there is a promising future for me at this organization.
I can achieve my career goals at this organization.

Macrodriver: Managers who recognize employees and mobilize their teams for peak performance
My manager provides me with recognition or praise for doing good work.
My manager treats me with dignity and respect.
My manager gives me useful feedback on how well I'm doing my job.
My manager is an effective listener.
My ideas and suggestions count.
The people I work with do their very best for the organization.

Macrodriver: Exciting work and the opportunity to improve skills
I get excited about my work.
My job makes good use of my skills and abilities.
My work gives me a feeling of personal accomplishment.
I am given a real opportunity to improve my skills at this organization.
This organization provides me with the opportunity for growth and development.
Overall, I am satisfied with the on-the-job training I have received.

Macrodriver: Organizations that demonstrate a genuine responsibility to their employees and communities
This organization supports employees' efforts to balance work and family/personal responsibilities.
Safety is a priority in my organization.
My organization's corporate social responsibility efforts have increased my overall satisfaction with working here.
My organization strives to serve the interests of multiple stakeholders (customers, employees, suppliers, and community), not just the shareholders.

WorkTrends database and my experience, I offer what is captured in Table 1.1 as a starting point in designing a well-founded employer-of-choice survey instrument.

Summary

Employer-of-choice surveys are the most commonly conducted surveys in organizations today. Most likely they are not referred to as "employer-of-choice" surveys, but the underlying purpose behind such survey programs is to tap into the notion of being a great place to work. The operating belief is that the quality of the work experience for employees will be important to both their engagement and their retention. This chapter discussed the concept of employee engagement and probed into both its drivers and the drivers of retention. The identification of these drivers suggests quite clearly the appropriate content of surveys aimed at this strategic business objective.

Chapter Five

Employee Surveys as Leading Indicators

Employee survey results can serve as leading indicators of business success. This is the most proactive, or "offensive," reason for conducting a survey and is becoming an increasingly common reason in the globalized, competitive marketplace. More management teams have come to believe not only that a more positive and engaged workforce will deliver stronger business performance, but that superior results can be achieved by understanding and taking action on employee survey-based leading indicators of business success. Still, this purpose for conducting an employee survey is in actual practice neither fully understood nor fully optimized. In this chapter, I provide a brief overview of the history of linkage research and its summary conclusions, outline and test the implications of these conclusions, and provide greater understanding of how surveys can be optimized as leading indicators.

The notion of using an employee survey as a leading indicator of business success is tied to linkage research (Wiley, 1996), which explores the relationship between how employees describe their work environment (as measured through an employee survey) and other critical success measures, such as customer satisfaction and business performance. The concept was first explored three decades ago by Benjamin Schneider and his colleagues (Schneider, Parkington, and Buxton, 1980), and since then, dozens of studies have been published demonstrating that employee survey ratings of the work environment are significantly correlated with customer satisfaction ratings, as well as an array of business performance measures. I presented a comprehensive summary of the research literature (Wiley, 1996) that resulted in the development of a linkage research model, later renamed the High Performance Model (Wiley and Campbell, 2006). Further research (Wiley and Brooks, 2000) produced a subsequent review of the literature and a taxonomy of the high performance organizational climate. High-profile studies (Heskett and others, 1994; Rucci, Kirn, and Quinn, 1998) have also demonstrated how employee surveys are leading indicators of organizational performance.

The High Performance Model

The High Performance Model (see Figure 5.1) integrated all previously published linkage research studies to produce a more comprehensive understanding than could be achieved by focusing on the results of any single linkage research study. The model suggests that the more present and visible certain organizational values and leadership practices are in a given work environment, the more energized, engaged, and productive is the workforce. The more energized, engaged, and productive the workforce, the greater are customer satisfaction and loyalty, and with a time lag, the stronger is the long-term business performance of the organization. More specifically, the High Performance Model describes how certain leadership practices (customer orientation, quality emphasis, training, and involvement) create positive results for employees. As employees perceive these practices as emphasized in their place of work, they align more with the goals of the organization, are more cooperative in their teamwork, are less likely to resign voluntarily, and have a higher level of employee engagement.

The High Performance Model describes how certain leadership practices (customer orientation, quality emphasis, training, and involvement) create positive results for employees.

Under these conditions, they can better deliver the organization's value proposition and thus achieve organizational goals.

Figure 5.1 High Performance Model

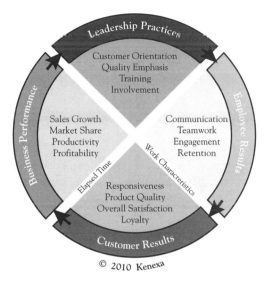

© 2010 Kenexa

A taxonomy of the high performance organizational climate was presented in the second major literature review (Wiley and Brooks, 2000). This taxonomy (see Table 5.1) was built on a blend of the original summary of the literature and a review of then recently published studies. Many of the newer studies were longitudinal in design and provided greater insight into the causal directions in the employee-customer-business performance linkages. This taxonomy, which has been modified slightly from its original presentation in order to be more precise, describes with greater clarity how high-performing units differ from low-performing units in the same organization. As with the High Performance Model, the taxonomy implies that these four leadership practices create an important set of positive employee results, which leads to higher customer satisfaction and loyalty that generates better business performance over time.

As I have noted elsewhere (Wiley, 2006), linkage research is a natural complement to other holistic models of organizational performance that emphasize leadership as the starting point.

Table 5.1 Taxonomy of the High Performance Organizational Climate

Customer orientation

- There is a strong emphasis on customer service, and the organization does a good job of satisfying customers.
- Customer needs are attended to quickly, whether in initial delivery of products and services or in the resolution of problems.

Quality emphasis

- Senior managers are committed to quality and demonstrate this priority in day-to-day decisions. These values are effectively translated and implemented by lower-level managers.
- Workers believe their groups deliver quality work as judged by clear quality standards, and they are able to improve continuously.

Training

- Workers have development plans and take advantage of available skill improvement opportunities.
- Workers are trained to perform their jobs well; this includes training on specific products and services or explicitly on customer service.
- New workers are oriented and able to come up to speed quickly without undue burden on existing staff.

Involvement

- Workers have the authority and support they need to serve their customers.
- Workers participate in decisions that affect their work and are encouraged to innovate.
- Managers solicit and use worker opinions and provide feedback on suggestions.

Communication

- Senior managers communicate a compelling vision and direction for the organization's future.
- Workers understand their role in the organization.
- Workers have the information needed to do their jobs, including information about the organization, advance warning of changes, and information from other departments.

Teamwork

- Workers both within and across functions cooperate to serve customers and get the work done; management actively supports teamwork.
- Workload is managed effectively within a given work group; the load is divided fairly, and short staffing is not a significant barrier.

Engagement

- Workers have confidence in the organization's ability to succeed, which leads to long-term stability and loyalty.
- Workers have pride in and are willing to advocate for their employer.
- Workers exert discretionary effort toward achieving group and organization goals.

Retention

- Workers value their relationship with the organization and have no short-term interest in leaving.
- Longer-tenured employees are especially valued; they are seen as more efficient and as creating more value for the organization and its customers.

Examples include the service profit chain (Heskett and others, 1994) and the balanced scorecard (Kaplan and Norton, 1996). The balanced scorecard, positioned by its creators as a vehicle for translating management strategy into action, connects leadership practices with its core interrelated business processes. The scorecard comprises leading and lagging indicators of performance and reflects the integrated systems that influence an organization's success or failure.

Viewed similarly, the High Performance Model outlines those leadership practices that most frequently and strongly drive employee results. Given this employee-customer-performance relationship, an employee survey featuring the High Performance Model dimensions positions an organization to diagnose its strengths and weaknesses in the cycle of performance. In ways unlike most other employee surveys, this approach situates the employee as an observer and reporter of the organization's leadership practices (that is, leading indicators) versus being a mere participant who rates satisfaction with various employee relations policies and practices. Thus, the employee is an ally in assessing how effectively the organization is delivering against its external value proposition. The results of this type of strategic measurement can be used as a stimulus to make needed correction in the implementation of strategy throughout the organization.

Implications for Survey Content

The original literature review of linkage research (Wiley, 1996) carried two strong implications for conducting employee surveys: one addressed survey content, and the other addressed how best to use survey results. This section focuses on the first of those two implications.

The High Performance Model and the review on which it is based suggest that decisions made about dimensions or topics included in an employee survey influence the probability that survey results will successfully predict outcome measures such as customer satisfaction and business performance, and thus qualify as a leading indicator. Four dimensions that measure the leadership practices component of the model have repeatedly shown the ability to predict outcome measures. These dimensions are customer orientation, quality emphasis, employee training, and involvement. Table 5.2 presents exemplar questions for each of these dimensions.

If the goal is to use survey results as leading indicators of business success, then the High Performance Model clearly implies that the survey content should contain the types of internal practice measures of organizational effectiveness displayed in Table 5.2. The more the survey contains these types of measures, the more likely it will be that the results will correlate positively and significantly with customer satisfaction and

Table 5.2 Exemplar Items for Leadership Practices

Customer orientation

- Where I work, customer problems are corrected quickly.
- Policies and procedures are designed to be user friendly to customers.
- There is a strong emphasis on customer service in this organization.
- We regularly use customer feedback to improve our processes.
- Overall, our customers are very satisfied with our products and services.

Quality emphasis

- We are continually improving the quality of our services.
- Leadership is committed to providing high-quality products and services to our external customers.
- Day-to-day decisions demonstrate that quality is a top priority.
- Where I work, we set clear performance standards for service quality.
- The people I work with deliver excellent quality and service.

Employee training

- New employees are given the training necessary to perform their jobs effectively.
- I receive the training I need to perform my current job effectively.
- Employees are getting the training they need to keep up with customer demands.
- I am given a real opportunity to improve my skills at this organization.
- This organization provides me with the opportunity for growth and development.

Involvement

- I have the authority to do what is necessary to effectively serve my customers.
- Employees are encouraged to participate in making decisions that affect their work.
- Sufficient effort is made to get the opinions and thinking of the people who work here.
- When employees have good ideas, management makes use of them.
- Employees are encouraged to be innovative, that is, to develop new and better ways of doing things.

business performance. The reason is that these practices set the tone for the organization by helping both leaders and employees understand what senior management regards as most important. This understanding and clarity create more confidence in senior leadership, facilitate better teamwork among employees, lead to lower voluntary resignation, and help create a more engaged workforce. All of these employee results position employees to be able to better deliver superior customer experiences and achieve performance objectives.

This implication can be tested with two case studies.

Case Study I

The setting for this case study is a large U.S.-based engineering and construction organization with multiple business units operating across the globe. The first worldwide employee survey was designed and implemented more than fifteen years ago. Through linkage research projects I have conducted with other clients, survey dimensions consistently emerged as the strongest correlates of customer satisfaction. These conclusions were shared with the client, and they expressed their desire that their survey program evolve to include more questions measuring the leadership practices outlined in the High Performance Model. The leadership team was also interested in validating the model in their context. The team requested that we integrate the two databases we maintained for them: the employee survey and the customer satisfaction survey databases. The customer satisfaction data were collected annually, and the employee survey data were collected every two years. For the linkage research we integrated the customer and employee survey data collected during the same calendar year.

A particular challenge in conducting linkage research for this client quickly became apparent. Aggregating data from the two distinct databases to a common level of analysis (a requirement for statistical linkage research) resulted in conducting linkage research on only eleven business units. In other words, since the unit of analysis by necessity had to be the global business unit, because that was the level at which the customer satisfaction data were collected, then size was limited to eleven. That necessitated using Spearman's rho, a rank order estimate of correlation.

When reviewing the customer survey results, the client gave special attention to the customer satisfaction index, which measured (1) satisfaction with the quality of the work performed, (2) how the work performed compared to that of the organization's competition, and (3) if the customer would consider the construction organization as the provider of the next project. This index was the key measure from the customer satisfaction survey on which the leadership team focused.

The employee survey was much longer: approximately fifty items subsumed under twelve employee survey dimensions. The organization routinely reviewed and discussed the results for all survey dimensions and items. However, for the purpose of this research, the leadership team wanted to create a special high performance index. A four-item index was proposed, with a single item from each of the four leadership practices of the High Performance Model:

1. The quickness of correcting customer problems, a measure of customer orientation

2. The comparative priority of quality of work versus the meeting of deadlines, a measure of quality emphasis

3. The extent to which new employees received the training necessary to perform their work effectively, a measure of training

4. Management's use of good ideas that employees suggested, a measure of involvement

The correlation coefficient between the employee survey-based high performance index and the customer satisfaction index was .69, statistically significant at p less than .05. In other words, there was a high and statistically significant relationship between the high performance and customer satisfaction indexes; units scoring high on one tended to score high on the other (see Figure 5.2). As a further test of the High Performance Model and its implications regarding the survey dimensions that are most predictive of customer satisfaction, all employee survey dimensions were correlated with the customer satisfaction index. The high performance index was the only employee survey measure that correlated significantly with the customer-satisfaction index.

From an organization development point of view, this finding also had great practical significance. The case study illustrates how an internal assessment, the employee survey, can predict customer satisfaction results quite accurately. Establishing this linkage was critical because this client's customer satisfaction index correlated with new project orders and revenue and thus predicted both top- and bottom-line financial results at the business unit level. As a result, how

How employees describe the organization can serve as a proxy for important measures of organizational success.

employees describe the organization can serve as a proxy for important measures of organizational success. In addition, this case study reveals how the employee survey results can identify gaps between the current state and the desired state of the organization and help the organization immensely in focusing organization development efforts for maximum gain.

Figure 5.2 Correlation of the High Performance and Customer Satisfaction Indexes

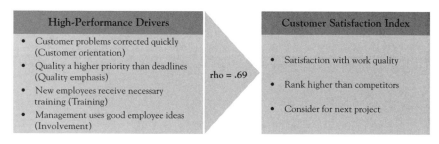

From a measurement perspective, the implication is clear. If the goal of the employee survey initiative is to serve as a leading indicator of business success, the survey should focus on measuring the leadership practices of the High Performance Model. These measures most frequently emerge as the strongest correlates of positive business outcomes, especially customer satisfaction and loyalty.

Case Study 2

The setting of this case study is a worldwide manufacturer of medical products. At the onset of the provider-client relationship, the organization expressed interest in using the employee survey as a measure of organizational effectiveness. This organization holds a strong belief that its employees are well informed and that if they are asked the appropriate questions about the quality of the manufactured products and the efficiency and effectiveness of its operations, the results will be extremely helpful in making the types of necessary adjustments to stay successful in a highly competitive industry.

Over the preceding decade, this organization had made major investments in a variety of quality initiatives: employee education and training, new production systems, new methods of measuring and ensuring quality, and a fierce commitment to continuous improvement. From a manufacturing perspective, this was its strategic focus. As a result, and to the credit of the thinking and rationale of the leadership team, they wanted a survey program that reflected this strategy: operational effectiveness, the highest possible quality, and an emphasis on continuous improvement.

At the same time, the organization also wanted to be an employer of choice in the communities in which it operated. It clearly believed that its ability to attract and retain top talent was essential and a core element of its future success. It had a long history of employee alignment with and support of the goals of the organization. It was, after all, in the business of producing products that both saved lives and enhanced the lives of patients. The leadership team featured these types of messages in recurring communications with employees. It was a clear part of the strategy to separate and differentiate itself from other employers competing for talent from the same labor pools.

Because of this employer-of-choice strategy, the leadership team also wanted to include in the employee survey topics known to be drivers of employee retention and central to building employer brand.

The leadership team described the employee survey program to the managers and employees as (1) a strategic business process to promote performance excellence, (2) aligned with their commitment to quality and longer-term strategic initiatives, and (3) a means of communicating the organization's core values. Furthermore, the program was to provide (1) results that identify leadership, management, and business practices that contribute to performance excellence and customer satisfaction; (2) information for driving change necessary to improve organizational effectiveness; (3) linkages to business performance; and (4) findings that identify organizational features and practices essential for attracting and retaining talent.

With this direction, an employee survey aimed at being both an employer-of-choice measurement and a leading indicator of business success was designed. The final survey contained seventy items measuring a broad array of dimensions: mission and strategy, customer orientation, quality emphasis, training, involvement, employee development, senior management, teamwork, job satisfaction, valuing employees, organization satisfaction, and employee retention.

Unlike case study 1, the client organization did not have a common method at the unit level of measuring customer satisfaction. Thus, it was not possible to include customer measures in an organization-wide linkage research study. The organization did, however, have financial performance data aggregated at a common level across business units and geographies. Consistent with the organization's emphasis on continuous improvement, its leaders chose to focus on revenue growth, computed as the cumulative revenue of the most recent four quarters divided by the cumulative revenue of the previous four quarters. Thus, revenue growth was a ratio, computed for each of the more than eighty business units included in this study.

To understand the work environment drivers of revenue growth, we focused on identifying survey items whose results most separated top- and bottom-revenue growth units. Thus, the scores for all survey items were computed for two groups of business units: the top quartile of units in revenue growth and the bottom quartile of units in revenue growth. Items that produced the ten largest gaps between the two groupings of business units were isolated. Of the ten items most separating top- and bottom-performing units, four items measured customer orientation, three items measured quality emphasis, and one item each measured training and involvement. The remaining item, showing one of the smallest gaps between top- and bottom-performing revenue growth units, measured pride and was part of the organization satisfaction dimension. The results of the analysis are presented in Figure 5.3.

As noted above, this client also had an employer-of-choice strategic objective. In its own terminology, the leaders referred to this as wanting to be a "best place to work." To understand better what influenced employee ratings of the organization as a best place to work, a special regression analysis of the item, "Considering everything, I am satisfied with this organization as a place to work," was conducted. The results are presented in Table 5.3.

This analysis indicates that it is the basic dynamics of the employer-employee relationship that most influence one's overall satisfaction with the organization. This includes the big-picture aspects of alignment with mission and trust in senior management, as well as the more day-to-day realities of what employees receive in exchange for their contributions in relation to work/life balance, benefits coverage, and opportunities for skill improvement and career development.

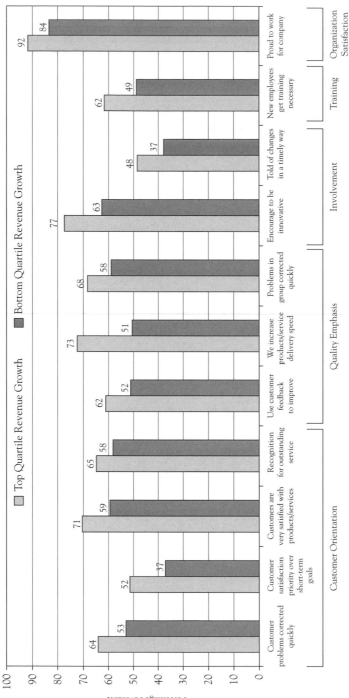

Figure 5.3 Survey Items That Most Differentiate High- and Low-Performing Units

Table 5.3 Survey Items Most Predictive of Organization Satisfaction

Dimension	Item(s)
Mission and strategic direction	The work I do supports the organization's mission.
Valuing employees	My organization supports me (programs, resources, flexibility, and so on) in having a healthy and balanced life. I am satisfied with my total benefits program.
Training	I have a real opportunity to improve my skills at my organization.
Senior management	Senior management supports and practices high standards of ethical conduct.
Employee development	I am satisfied with the career development opportunities at my organization.

Case Study Discussion

In part, these two case studies were selected for inclusion in this chapter because of their uniqueness. Linkage research ers readily acknowledge the difficulty of conducting linkage research in industries such as manufacturing and construction. A major obstacle often cited is the inability to obtain outcome measures such as customer satisfaction and business performance at a common level of aggregation (the business unit level). This was illustrated in case study 2; the client organization did not have a common measure of customer service or satisfaction or loyalty across the organization's many business units. In this case, the obstacle was overcome by linking the employee perspective directly to the financial perspective without exploring the intervening contribution of the customer experience.

Another major obstacle often cited in these types of industries is an insufficient number of units for conducting linkage research. Because linkage research treats the organizational unit (instead of the individual employee) as the unit of analysis, it is sometimes difficult to obtain a sufficient number of units to perform the type of analysis most typically relied on (Pearson correlation analysis) in conducting linkage research. This was illustrated in case study 1; the client had only eleven global business units for which the two available databases were aggregated at a common level. The obstacle was overcome by using an alternative method of measuring the degree of relationship: Spearman's rho coefficient, a rank-order method of computing correlation.

Branch banking and retail organizations are much more likely candidates for linkage research because they can treat branches or retail outlets as the unit of analysis. All three measures—employee, customer, and financial—are often available in these organizational settings. This is why linkage research publications are disproportionately representative of these types of service industries.

Despite these realities, the much more important part of the case study discussion has to do with the implications for survey content. In both case studies, the results for all items included in each of the two employee surveys had an equal opportunity to demonstrate a significant and meaningful relationship to the outcome measures under consideration. In both cases, however, it was clear that the items that measured certain leadership practices emerged as either the strongest correlates, or the only correlates, of the customer or financial outcome under consideration. These leadership practices are customer orientation, quality emphasis, training, and involvement.

This illustrates and reinforces the point made by the linkage research results summarized in the High Performance Model: if the goal of the survey is to use its results as a leading indicator of downstream success, whether that success is in the customer experience or in financial performance, it behooves the organization to incorporate into the survey dimensions and items that research has shown to be the strongest correlates or predictors of those outcomes. In this sense, not all employee survey items are equal. Some simply emerge more frequently and more strongly as enjoying the most potent relationships with customer satisfaction and loyalty and financial performance.

> *It behooves the organization to incorporate into the survey dimensions and items that research has shown to be the strongest correlates or predictors of those outcomes.*

Summary

As I noted earlier (Wiley, 1996), this conclusion regarding the survey dimensions that are the most potent predictors of business outcomes does not mean that measuring other dimensions is not worthwhile. Consistent with one of the primary theses of this book, this does mean that it is critically important to be clear about purpose. When there is clarity of purpose for the survey program because it is aligned with overarching strategic objectives, decisions about survey content are more easily made. When a survey's primary purpose is to serve as a leading indicator of business performance and success, measuring the orientation toward serving the customer, the value placed on the quality of products and services, and the extent to which workers feel properly trained to do their jobs and are involved in decision making that affects their work should be centrally featured in the survey's content. If you want the survey to be a predictor of downstream organization effectiveness, ask employees about those aspects of their work environment that either facilitate or serve as an obstacle to getting their work done and serving their customers better.

Chapter Six

Merging Employer-of-Choice and Leading-Indicator Survey Purposes

The Strategic Survey Model was first presented at a professional conference (Wiley and Weiner, 2002) and subsequently published a few years later (Wiley, 2006). Even prior to its publication, the model was used to guide clients' conceptualization of the employee survey strategy as well as the subsequent development of the survey content that would fulfill their strategy. As clients considered the implications of the model, it often became amazingly clear to them what they really wanted. For example, they may have thought that their purpose was about being a great place to work. If so, they needed a survey tool that would help them retain and engage their workforce. When they articulated that objective, it was obvious they were aligning with the employer-of-choice survey type.

Increasingly for many clients, measuring employer-of-choice topics was not enough. Perhaps driven by strong marketplace competition on issues of customer service or quality, or operating from a fundamental belief in their employees being extremely well-informed about operational issues, clients began asking for a hybrid survey program. They wanted a measure that would help them retain and engage their workforce and at the same time give them keen insights into the operational side of their delivery system. In other words, their business strategy was best served by a measurement program combining employer-of-choice and leading-indicator survey types.

In addition, these clients were also asking for a model of how the two survey types aligned with their corporate objectives. One client, a major U.S. retail clothing chain, developed a graphic display of its perspective (a revised version is presented in Figure 6.1).

Figure 6.1 Clear Survey Purpose and Goals

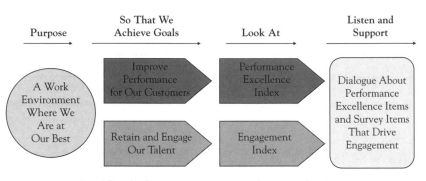

If we follow this flow, we stay on purpose and meet our objectives

This client wanted to be as clear as possible in its communication with several layers of managers throughout this organization. The graphic focused everyone's ideas of what the survey program was about: becoming a work environment where all coworkers are "at their best." That would allow them to achieve their twin goals of "improving performance for our customers" (a leading-indicator type of survey purpose) and "retaining and engaging our talent" (an employer-of-choice type of survey purpose). This led to the development of two survey indexes, comprising a total of eleven items on which they would focus. The first index is a performance excellence index, with items derived from the High Performance Model (see Chapter Five). Research has shown that these items have a strong predictive relationship to actual customer service measures. The second index is the employee engagement index, with items that measure the components of engagement as outlined in Chapter Four: pride, satisfaction, commitment, and advocacy. This index has also been positively correlated to business performance. A listing of the items comprising these two indexes is presented in Table 6.2 near the end of the chapter.

The guidance given to the managers of this organization was to focus their primary survey and feedback efforts on these two indexes. In the case of the performance excellence index, that meant understanding why employees rated the items on the index as they did and taking the necessary actions to lift the scores on those items. In the case of the employee engagement index, managers were to focus on the priorities of employee engagement, that is, the ten items in the survey whose results had the strongest relationship to the employee engagement index. Again, the fundamental notion is to generate an understanding of why employees rate the engagement priorities the way they do and develop responsive actions to lift those scores as measured on subsequent surveys. This in turn would have the natural effect of improving the overall employee engagement index score.

In the broader sense, many clients are becoming increasingly vocal that they want to achieve, strategically, two complementary goals: creating a high performance organization and building an engaged workforce. In this sense, the two constructs of performance excellence and employee engagement are complementary, that is, they serve to fill out, or complete, or mutually supply each other's lack. Consider Figure 6.2, which focuses on the interplay between a high performance organization and an engaged workforce. The fundamental idea is that the organization will best meet its performance targets and deliver its value

Figure 6.2 Maximizing Success

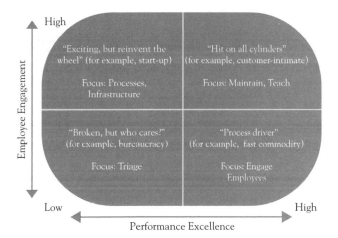

proposition to its customers under the conditions of achieving both performance excellence and employee engagement.

In some respects, this notion may seem obvious. Despite that, for many organizations it is only in the recent past that they have begun to articulate their understanding of the distinction between these two objectives. Being able to see the distinction leads them quite naturally to a survey strategy that reflects both concepts.

The two constructs of performance excellence and employee engagement are complementary.

Consider Figure 6.3 as a way to capture the needful and harmonious combination of these two constructs. In this metaphor, performance excellence is the engine that ultimately drives performance. Its design is based on certain engineering specifications and features aimed to produce measurable outcomes. And employee engagement is the fuel. To produce the best outcomes and performance, it also must meet certain engineering specifications and requirements. It supplies the energy necessary to power the engine; it is what actuates the organization.

**Figure 6.3 A Metaphor for Performance Excellence
and Employee Engagement**

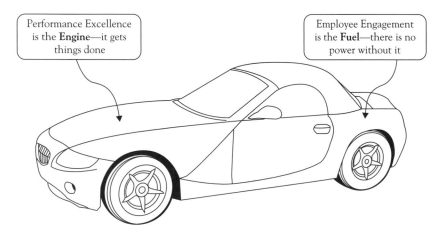

Performance Excellence
is the **Engine**—it gets
things done

Employee Engagement
is the **Fuel**—there is no
power without it

In reality, both constructs, performance excellence and employee engagement, have rich streams of research history demonstrating their relationship to desirable organizational outcomes. When their power as predictors is compared, performance excellence typically emerges as the stronger predictor of customer service and business growth outcomes, while employee engagement emerges as the stronger predictor of organizational commitment and employee retention. However, as illustrated by the engine-fuel metaphor of Figure 6.3, both are necessary. In fact, it is their conceptual differentiation and synergistic interaction that produces optimal results.

The High Performance–Engagement Model

When leaders support both performance excellence and employee engagement, organizational performance is at its highest. The performance excellence and employee engagement indexes serve as proxies of actual performance outcomes because of their known positive relationships to measures of business performance. This view of organizational performance is captured in Figure 6.4, which introduces the High Performance–Engagement Model.

> *The performance excellence and employee engagement indexes serve as proxies of actual performance outcomes because of their known positive relationships to measures of business performance.*

The model recognizes that organizations often articulate the two complementary goals of becoming a high performance organization and developing and sustaining an engaged workforce. The research (see Chapters Four and Five for background) establishes the leadership requirements needed to achieve both of these goals. In the case of the high performance organization, leadership supports the practices of customer orientation, quality emphasis, training, and involvement. In the case of the engaged workforce, leadership models and reinforces the behaviors that build confidence and trust, demonstrate recognition and respect, support growth

Figure 6.4 The High Performance–Engagement Model

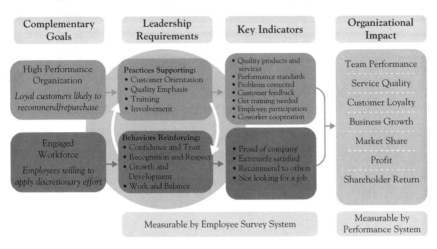

and development, and ensure that workers are placed in roles that match well with their skills and interests.

Obviously an employee survey can be built to measure the extent to which these practices and behaviors are reflected in the workplace. As noted previously, the key indicators are the items comprising the performance excellence and employee engagement indexes. Both indexes have a record of predicting the organizational impacts listed in Figure 6.4. However, to maximize performance, both sets of leadership requirements must be practiced and reinforced. In other words, these practices and behaviors interact to lead the organization to greater success than a concentration on either one of the goals alone could produce.

Validation of the High Performance–Engagement Model

Building a model is one thing; demonstrating its validity is another. To validate this model, the ability of the performance excellence index (PEI) and the employee engagement index (EEI) is examined independently, additively, and interactively to predict important business outcomes. While the independent relationships of the two indexes to business outcomes has already been documented, the challenge is to show, consistent with the assertions of the High Performance–Engagement Model, how these two indexes in combination and interactively relate more strongly to business outcomes than does either construct independently. The model is validated in a three-step process.

Step One: Establishing the Relationship of the PEI and the EEI to the Outcome Indicator

The WorkTrends database was used to correlate the PEI and EEI to an employee-based measure of organizational success labeled the *performance outcome indicator*. The rationale is this: employees' perceptions of important organizational practices provide valuable insights into how well an operation is functioning. Previous research (Schneider and Bowen, 1985) has demonstrated that employees' ratings of organizational practices and procedures correlate highly and significantly with the perceptions of external stakeholders. Thus, employee perceptions of customer service and quality can serve as a proxy for actual ratings of customer satisfaction and unit productivity. Adopting that notion to measure employees' perceptions of overall customer service, quality, and organizational performance, the performance outcome indicator is employed. It has four items:

- My organization provides higher-quality products and services than other similar organizations do.
- Overall, customers are very satisfied with the products and services they receive from my organization.
- My organization competes well against others in the industry.
- My organization's performance has improved performance during the past year.

Consistent with one of the primary implications of the High Performance–Engagement Model—that the performance excellence and employee engagement indexes are significantly related to performance outcomes—it was found that the PEI ($r = .78$) and the EEI ($r = .68$) are indeed highly and significantly related to the performance outcome indicator. It is expected that tangible organizational practices such as good customer service and consistent high-quality products will have a positive impact on overall performance and organizational competitiveness, but perhaps the relationship between employee engagement and this type of performance outcome measure is not as intuitive. Common perceptions dictate that the constructs of performance excellence and employee engagement are different and separate—perhaps the hard and soft side of an organization, respectively. In actuality, this research demonstrates that the PEI and EEI are highly related to each other ($r = .72$), which indicates that employee perceptions of their organization's customer service, quality of products, and employee involvement and training matter to employee engagement and vice versa.

Step Two: Establishing the Additive Power of PEI and EEI in Predicting Organizational Financial Success

The next focus is the impact of the PEI and EEI on financial metrics. Leadership and organizational efforts invested in improving performance excellence and employee engagement are an exercise in futility if they do not lead to the achievement of important organizational goals. Clearly it is the outcomes of performance excellence and employee engagement that matter to an organization.

To examine the combined impact of the performance excellence and employee engagement constructs on fiscal business metrics, we explored their relationship to three-year total shareholder return (TSR). This was measured by coupling publicly reported TSR data for 158 organizations with WorkTrends data derived from employees in those same organizations. The organizations represent all major industries, including retail, financial services and banking, health care products, and services in all major geographies. Eighty-five percent of the organizations are multinational, with locations and employees in more than one hundred countries. The majority of these organizations

(80 percent) have more than ten thousand employees. Approximately 8 percent are Fortune 100 organizations, and 30 percent are Fortune 500 organizations.

This research presents a few major challenges; most important of these is the reality that many factors contribute to an organization's three-year TSR, including market forces and investor perceptions, elements that are not entirely under the control of organizational leaders. Nevertheless, as hypothesized by the High Performance–Engagement Model, both the PEI ($r = .18$) and the EEI ($r = .19$) were positively and significantly related to three-year TSR.

The analyses further indicated that the combined contribution of performance excellence and employee engagement accounts for almost 4 percent of an organization's three-year TSR. This is a notably greater contribution to understanding the influencers of three-year TSR than could be provided by a focus on the PEI or EEI alone. Furthermore, while this percentage may seem small, it is actually a significant contribution to understanding what influences three-year TSR.

These results also mirror the conclusion from step 1: performance excellence and employee engagement are significantly, uniquely, and equally important to an organization's overall business performance. This noteworthy finding tells us that leaders and managers should work to improve both indexes in tandem as a path to stronger organizational financial performance. In fact, organizations focusing solely on either of these individual constructs alone run the risk of suboptimizing, failing to grasp opportunities for positive impacts on their fiscal health.

Step Three: Establishing the Interactive Power of PEI × EEI in Predicting Organizational Financial Success

In steps 1 and 2, the positive impact of performance excellence and employee engagement was demonstrated, independently and in combination, on business performance metrics. The High Performance–Engagement Model also depicts that the leadership requirements for building a high performance organization and an engaged workforce in combination produce a reinforcing, compounding interactive effect. This means that the leadership practices that help build a high performance organization also help create an engaged workforce and that the leadership behaviors that reinforce the creation of an engaged workforce help in building a high performance organization. In step 3, in addition to examining the independent and combined contributions of each construct to business performance, the multiplicative effect of the two constructs in tandem is explored (see Figure 6.5).

> *The leadership practices that help build a high performance organization also help create an engaged workforce.*

To investigate the compounded or multiplicative effects of the High Performance–Engagement Model, the same sample of 158 organizations previously described was used, this time to investigate the impact of performance excellence multiplied by the impact of employee engagement on diluted earnings per share (DEPS), an important financial performance metric to investors for organizational stock evaluation. Beyond indicating margin and stock evaluation health, DEPS is a standardized metric that reflects an organization's ability to increase revenue,

Figure 6.5 The Synergistic Effect of Performance Excellence and Employee Engagement Multiplied

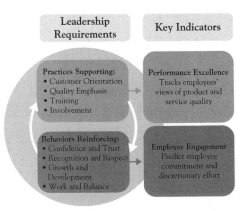

satisfy customers, and effectively and efficiently deliver its products or services as a means to creating profitability.

After first establishing that the PEI ($r = .19$) and the EEI ($r = .27$) are positively and significantly related to DEPS, their combined impact was explored. The analysis revealed that, together, the constructs of performance excellence and employee engagement account for a substantial 7.8 percent of the variance in DEPS. This corroborates the analysis summarized in step 2 pertaining to three-year TSR. The same conclusion is reached: the combination of performance excellence and employee engagement more strongly relates to important business performance metrics than either construct does independently.

Figure 6.6 expresses the relationship between PEI + EEI and DEPS in another way. The average DEPS for two groups—those organizations with PEI and EEI scores placing them in the top 25 percent of the study group and those with respective index scores placing them in the bottom 25 percent—are calculated. The comparison of these two groups reveals that the higher the PEI and EEI scores, the stronger the DEPS. Stated differently, organizations with employees reporting combined high PEI and EEI scores achieve more than two and a half times greater DEPS than organizations whose employees report combined low PEI and EEI scores.

Figure 6.6 The Effect of Performance Excellence Index and Employee Engagement Index on Diluted Earnings per Share

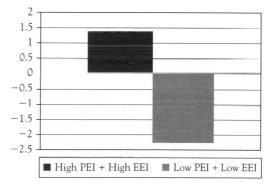

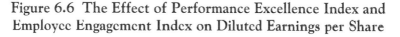

The next sequential test of the High Performance–Engagement Model, and the real purpose of step 3, is to examine the multiplicative effect of performance excellence and employee engagement. Analyses reveal that the multiplicative effect improves the ability to explain DEPS, adding 1.6 percent to the amount of variance for which the two constructs account. In total, almost 10 percent of DEPS (9.4 percent, to be exact) is accounted for by the combined and multiplied influences of the performance excellence and employee engagement indexes. This is an important finding because it tells us that a substantial amount of an organization's DEPS is understood when the PEI and EEI scores are known. Because what comprises the PEI and what drives the EEI are known, leaders and managers now have available a potent arrow in their quiver for enhancing their organization's DEPS.

A summary of the relationships between the constructs of performance excellence and employee engagement and the three business performance metrics is presented in Table 6.1. This summary provides clear and substantial support for the model.

Table 6.1 Summary of the Relationship Between Performance Excellence Index Plus the Employee Engagement Index and Business Performance Metrics

Performance Metric	Metric Significantly Related to:		PEI + EEI: Combination Explains More Performance Metric Variance than Either Construct Alone	PEI × EEI: Interactive Effect Further Increases Performance Metric Variance Explained
	PEI	EEI		
Outcome indicator	Yes	Yes	Yes	No[a]
Three-year TSR	Yes	Yes	Yes	Yes[b]
Diluted earnings	Yes	Yes	Yes	Yes

[a]The variance explained already stands at an extremely high 63 percent.

[b]The interactive effect increases the variance explained, but the net gain is not statistically significant at the $p \geq .1$ level.

As posited by the High Performance–Engagement Model, the summary reveals the following:

- As independent constructs, both performance excellence and employee engagement are significantly and positively related to all three performance metrics.
- The combination of the performance excellence and employee engagement constructs is more strongly related to, and provides a deeper explanation of, all three performance metrics than either construct alone.
- In the two cases involving a financial performance metric, the interactive effect of performance excellence and employee engagement adds to the explanation of the metric, beyond the explanation provided by either construct alone or by the two constructs combined. The one case where this is not true is the employee perception-based outcome indicator, where the amount of variance accounted for is already extremely high (63 percent).

The goal of developing and introducing the new High Performance–Engagement Model is twofold: (1) to update and codify the science and logic undergirding the use of employee surveys as predictors of business success and (2) to provide practitioners and executive sponsors of employee survey programs with a fuller understanding of how to use survey research technology as a tool for building stronger organizations, capable of performing at higher levels. By measuring and targeting improvements for both fundamental constructs depicted in the High Performance–Engagement Model—performance excellence and employee engagement—organizations can have a positive effect on individual and unit productivity, customer satisfaction and loyalty, and bottom-line financial results.

Implications of the High Performance–Engagement Model on Survey Content

I always recommend that survey content be matched to clear organizational objectives and well-articulated management information needs. With that acknowledgment, if an organization identifies with the High Performance–Engagement Model as capturing its strategic employee survey objectives, a starting place for survey content is listed in Table 6.2.

As seen from Table 6.2, the survey content that matches the model is relatively easy to develop or to select from a bank of survey items. Indeed, there is some overlap between the content associated with the high performance organization and the content associated with the drivers of employee engagement, but the

Table 6.2 High Performance–Engagement Model Dimensions and Illustrative Survey Items

Supporting Leadership Practices

Customer orientation

We regularly use customer feedback to improve our processes.

Customer problems get corrected quickly.

There is a strong emphasis on customer service in this organization.

Quality emphasis

Leadership is committed to providing high-quality products and services to external customers.

Where I work, we set clear performance standards for product and service quality.

Day-to-day decisions demonstrate that quality and improvement are top priorities.

Training

I receive the training I need to perform my current job effectively.

New employees receive the training necessary to perform their jobs effectively.

Employees are getting the training they need to keep up with customer demands.

Involvement

Employees are encouraged to participate in making decisions that affect their work.

My ideas and suggestions count.

The people I work with cooperate to get the job done.

Reinforcing Leadership Behaviors

Confidence and trust

I have confidence in the future of this organization.

The leaders of this organization have communicated a vision of the future that motivates me.

I trust the leaders of this organization.

Growth and development

I can achieve my career goals at this organization.

I feel there is a promising future for me at this organization.

My manager has made a personal investment in my growth and development.

Performance excellence index[a]

We regularly use customer feedback to improve our processes.

Customer problems get corrected quickly.

Leadership is committed to providing high-quality products and services to external customers.

Where I work, we set clear performance standards for product and service quality.

Employees are getting the training they need to keep up with customer demands.

Employees are encouraged to participate in making decisions that affect their work.

The people I work with cooperate to get the job done.

Recognition and respect

My manager provides me with recognition or praise for doing good work.

My manager treats me with dignity and respect.

My manager is an effective listener.

Work and balance

I get excited about my work.

My job makes good use of my skills and abilities.

This organization supports employees' efforts to balance work and family/personal responsibilities.

Employee engagement index

I am proud to tell people I work for my organization.

Overall, I am extremely satisfied with my organization as a place to work.

I rarely think about looking for a new job with another organization.

I would recommend this place to others as a good place to work.

Note: Twenty-eight items are needed to reliably measure the High Performance–Engagement Model.

[a]The PEI comprises seven items drawn from four different dimensions.

overlap is relatively minimal. Taking into consideration the inclusion of the separate four-item employee engagement index, and that the performance excellence index is built into the dimensions suggested by the model, Table 6.2 displays how the measurement of the High Performance–Engagement Model can be captured in a survey containing only twenty-eight items.

Summary

This chapter closes Part One of this book. Its intent was to introduce the Strategic Survey Model and to describe in Chapters One through Five each of the four levels of the model: using employee surveys as warning indicators, program evaluation measures, measures of employer of choice, and leading indicators of organizational performance. This chapter introduced a hybrid purpose: combining into one survey program both the employer of choice and the leading indicator employee survey purposes. That produced the High Performance–Engagement Model, as well as recommended survey content that converts the model into an actual survey instrument.

Part Two moves beyond measurement and addresses the other key to a successful survey program: effectively using the results of an employee survey. Chapter Seven introduces and discusses some of the most basic and important ideas of survey feedback and action planning. Chapter Eight reviews some techniques that support the employee survey results goal-setting process. Chapter Nine discusses the leadership requirements for sustaining improvement over time in survey results. Finally, Chapter Ten summarizes key messages of Part Two and provides some final thoughts.

Part Two

Survey Follow-up

Chapter Seven

An Overview of Survey Feedback and Action Planning

The primary goal of an employee survey program is to produce tangible and lasting organizational improvements. For many experienced survey practitioners, a common belief is that in successful survey programs, 20 percent of the total survey effort falls into planning, developing, and administering the actual survey and tabulating and reporting its results. The remaining 80 percent of the effort expended by the organization falls into the survey follow-up. If those estimates are even close to being true, it is obvious that the quality of the follow-up process is critical to overall employee survey program success.

I have found it easier to guide organizations through a survey follow-up process if they operate according to a model, or a flow. This allows an organization to know where it is starting and where it is headed. Several years ago, I developed the seven-step model presented in Figure 7.1. This model is the application of

Figure 7.1 The Seven-Step Model for Survey Feedback and Action Planning

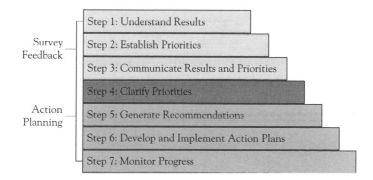

Survey Feedback

Step 1: Understand Results
Step 2: Establish Priorities
Step 3: Communicate Results and Priorities

Action Planning

Step 4: Clarify Priorities
Step 5: Generate Recommendations
Step 6: Develop and Implement Action Plans
Step 7: Monitor Progress

the fundamental philosophies of organizational development to employee survey methodology.

In this chapter, I briefly describe each step of the model but give more attention to the philosophy of the model and less attention to actual techniques and processes. My purpose is to describe how organizations should think about survey follow-up, not to provide a miniature step-by-step guide for follow-up and action planning.

Step One: Understand Results

Before an organization or a manager of an individual unit can effectively communicate survey results and take action, there needs to be an understanding of what the results reveal. The basic idea is to arrive at an understanding of the strengths and opportunities for improvement. In some cases, this understanding may come through a presentation provided by a subject matter survey expert, either internal or external to the organization. In other cases, individual managers are responsible for reviewing the results for their own department or organizational unit and drawing the proper conclusions. Guidelines or formulas can be used to define strength and opportunity for improvement. Often normative data—in the best cases, industry or geographical normative comparisons—are available to help place survey results into context. While normative comparisons are often viewed as highly valuable, the best point of comparison is, in my estimation, historical survey results. Trend lines indicate whether a specific organization is making progress, standing still, or declining. Although there is no substitute for a thorough analysis of survey results, in developing an understanding of what survey results reveal, the real focus should be on the pattern of the data and the total picture they create. Organizations can waste

Organizations can waste precious time and energy when they overanalyze results.

precious time and energy when they overanalyze results and focus on organizational, normative, or even trend comparisons of minor consequence.

Step Two: Establish Priorities

All steps of the seven-step model are important, but two of them distinguish successful from unsuccessful survey follow-up efforts. The first is establishing priorities. Many organizations make the mistake of trying to work on too many priorities. This mistake is based on the myth that employees expect action on every critical issue emerging from the survey results. They do not (they are much smarter than that). What they do expect is that their organization will respond to a few of the more important issues. At the managerial level, those issues are the priorities that managers have control over, not policy-level issues such as the benefits the organization may offer.

Obviously organizational resources are finite. Organizations whose follow-up efforts focus on a short list of priorities are usually more satisfied with the follow-up outcomes than those that have a longer nonprioritized list. It is therefore critical to focus on the survey-based priorities deemed to be of greatest consequence. I typically advise clients to work on only two or three priorities. Establishing priorities by choosing a strength to maintain and one or two opportunities to improve helps balance actions for improvement by focusing on both positive and negative results.

There are a number of ways to establish priorities:

- At the total organizational level, a facilitator can lead an executive team through a guided discussion aimed at establishing alignment within the group regarding the top priorities emerging from the survey results. For example, I used this method with a leading financial services industry organization. After presenting the results, I led the team through a modified nominal group process, which resulted in agreement on the three priorities that would be the focus of follow-up action planning processes.

- When an organization is focused on a particular index, for example, employee engagement, it can use statistical techniques, such as correlation, regression, or even relative weights analysis, to help establish key priorities for follow-up. Identifying the correlates of a key measure illuminates the most important areas for follow-up. When improvements are achieved in areas of high impact, the natural and typical consequence is improvement in the key index under consideration. This technique can be employed at the organization, department, or organizational unit level (assuming the respondent sample size at the unit level is sufficient for this type of statistical analysis).

- At the department or organizational unit level, managers can establish priorities after studying their own reports of survey results. They may also do this after reviewing and discussing the results with other managers in their unit. This deserves a special note: management's determination of priorities without further employee input is a legitimate technique for establishing priorities. Employees have already been involved in the survey process (after all, it is their survey results that are under consideration) and will continue to be involved at key stages in the survey process, including the later steps of clarifying priorities and generating recommendations for improvement.

- In some organizations that place a high priority on employee involvement in establishing priorities, management can create a list of four to five potential priorities and invite employees to shorten that list. Management then reviews and approves the final list of priorities.

Regardless of the technique employed for establishing priorities, organizations that do this well have successfully navigated around one of the biggest pitfalls in effective survey follow-up processes: having too many priorities on which to work. A list of priorities that outmatches the resources or resolve of the organization almost always leads to employee cynicism toward and distrust of the process. A short list of priorities worked well will advance the cause of the organization much better and faster than a long list worked poorly. The same 80/20 rule should apply; focus on the 20 percent that can make 80 percent of the difference, and rewards will follow. When organizations put effective action plans in place, this invariably lifts the overall profile of results on the subsequent survey, even lifting dimensions that were not the focus of action planning efforts.

> *One of the biggest pitfalls in effective survey follow-up processes [is] having too many priorities on which to work.*

Step Three: Communicate Results and Priorities

Survey results should be communicated to employees as soon as practicable after the results become available. Ideally results are presented to the leadership team of an organization, who then establish a short list of survey-based priorities for action planning. When that happens, a company-wide memo from the top leadership of the organization (preferably from the CEO) should communicate to employees:

- Thanks for their participation in the survey process
- The survey response rate
- A short list of major strengths and opportunities for improvement
- If available, a brief reference to trend results

- Priorities the leadership team has established
- How employees will be involved in survey feedback and action planning processes

Managers receiving reports of survey results for their own organizational unit have an important communication responsibility. In fact, I advise organizations that the decision to provide individual managers with reports of survey results is equivalent to that manager's having a responsibility to feed back results to employees and involve them in developing responsive action plans.

In preparing for employee feedback meetings, managers must make decisions about how much they will accomplish in a meeting. To work through the whole process, they need to present the results to employees, clarify the results with them (see step 4), and then develop the action plan (see steps 5 and 6). Especially with larger groups, it is not possible to accomplish all of these steps in one meeting. Typically the first purpose can be achieved at the initial meeting, along with an announcement as to how steps 4 though 6 will be achieved.

Although this chapter does not focus on technique, a few fundamental practices are important for those who conduct feedback sessions with employees:

- Select communication techniques that fit the organization. As much as possible, employees should see the feedback and action planning process as part of how the organization normally conducts business (for example, through regularly scheduled staff meetings) versus creating entirely new communication processes.
- Match the presentations of results to the audience and the appropriate level of detail. It is typical, especially for those leading the process for the first time, to present too much information. Most employees will be satisfied with a

This example illustrates that one of the biggest mistakes organizations can make in the use of employee survey results is to leap from a raw, first-cut understanding of the quantitative results to the prescription of solutions (that is, action plans) without first coming to an understanding of the root cause. Unfortunately a trend I have experienced in my career is that the higher the managerial level, the more frequent the leap.

Figure 7.2 shows that survey results serve the purpose of educating and informing management regarding what employees are thinking. Involving employees in a dialogue around the survey results in feedback meetings or focus group interviews is necessary to determine why employees feel the way they do. The "what" and the "why" constitute survey feedback. It is not until both sets of information are available—the quantitative survey results and the qualitative employee-based clarification of results—that the organization is in a position to know how it can or should respond.

Involving employees in a dialogue around the survey results in feedback meetings or focus group interviews is necessary to determine why employees feel the way they do.

The clarifying dialogue can be highly tailored to a specific set of results or more generic. In a general sense, the types of questions that stimulate the root

Figure 7.2 Clarifying Survey Results: What, Why, and How

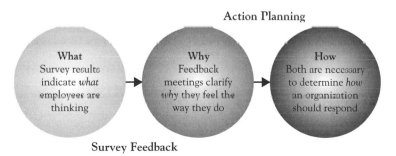

cause discussion deal directly with survey results and can be as simple as asking:

- Why do employees feel this way? What causes the opinion?
- Whom does the issue affect?
- When [or how often] does this occur?
- What's the impact on the performance of the group?
- What are ideas or recommendations for how the issue can be addressed, fixed, or improved?

Step Five: Generate Recommendations

Many approaches to generating recommendations have proven successful. As the last question in the list implies, this step is another opportunity to involve employees in the process. Approaches that have proven successful include using employees to generate recommendations for improvement at the end of clarification meetings or at a later meeting or putting together action planning teams assigned to work on a given priority. There are occasions, based on the type of priority, when managers or management teams are the ones best suited for generating recommendations. Decisions regarding how to tailor the process are influenced by how unit priorities may overlap or be integrated with organization-wide priorities or the extent to which priorities align with existing strategic planning or other organization development activities.

Once recommendations have been generated, the ideas themselves must be evaluated for fit, impact, and efficacy. In evaluating potential solutions, it is important to consider how directly the proposed actions are to the specific survey items or dimensions the organization hopes to improve. A good test to apply is to ask, "How confident am I that this action, if successfully implemented, will improve the survey results for the targeted items or dimensions the next time we survey?"

Step Six: Develop and Implement Action Plans

Once there is agreement on the best recommendations for addressing the action planning priorities, these recommendations must be converted into actions. Specific objectives should be established that support each overall action plan. The most successful action plans should contain objectives that are specific and easily understood; measurable, thus allowing progress to be monitored; achievable; and compatible, that is, contributing to the mission and goals of the group but in no way working against other key objectives.

The action planning process, regardless of the techniques through which it was developed, needs to specify these components:

- *Steps.* What is required to reach the objective?
- *Timing.* When will it be accomplished?
- *Assistance needed.* What resources or information are required to meet the objective?
- *Responsibility.* Who will do what?

Once created, action plans will continue to require time and effort to ensure they are implemented successfully. Through my experience, I have identified several facilitators of action plan success. One is to be as specific as possible in defining the issue. Another is to identify a concrete first step, that is, one that clearly reflects the transition from planning to doing. In some cases, it is useful to start with some easily accomplished objectives. This builds both momentum for the action planning process and trust among employees that the organization is serious about using survey results to affect change. Finally, as organizations prepare to implement their plans, they should ask, "What could lead this plan to fail, and how will we know when the situation is improved?" The answer to the second of those two questions is addressed in step seven.

Step Seven: Monitor Progress

To monitor progress, an organization must have both methods of tracking and processes for reporting and discussing progress. With regard to tracking progress, the ultimate method is through the results of a subsequent survey. There is more to say about that in the next chapter on goal setting. Depending on the objectives under consideration, though, there may be other, more readily available measures. For example, if actions are undertaken to increase employee engagement and lower voluntary turnover, then tracking voluntary turnover rates provides a measure of progress. And if actions are undertaken to increase customer loyalty through strengthening the customer orientation culture of the organization, customer loyalty and satisfaction ratings provide highly relevant progress measures.

Monitoring progress also requires processes for reporting and discussing progress. Action plan progress can be reported and discussed in these ways:

- An individual performance review process, under the circumstances where individuals have responsibilities for action implementation.
- Unit-level operations reviews, where progress on other key organizational initiatives and performance objectives are discussed.
- Regular meetings involving employees, such as staff, communication meetings, or town hall meetings. Although these employee meetings may seem more like opportunities for simply reporting progress, the fact that such a report needs to be made unleashes energy useful toward action plan completion.

The final point about communication that needs to be stressed deals with the occasion when effective actions are developed and implemented but not communicated to employees. I refer to this as a failure to merchandise. Failure to keep employees informed of how their input is being used to change the organization can be, and often is, a serious problem in achieving the greatest gain from a survey feedback organization development process.

Effective communication of action plans builds a true sense of employee involvement and participation. In organizations where this practice is implemented, employees have a much more positive feeling about the effectiveness of survey feedback as a tool for organization change, and correspondingly, leaders and managers come to realize the full potential of what the survey feedback organization development process can achieve.

Summary

The primary goal of an employee survey program is to produce tangible and lasting organizational improvements. It is easier for organizations to achieve this goal if they follow a disciplined survey follow-up process. In this chapter, I offer a seven-step survey feedback and action planning model.

Every organization is unique. Survey content and follow-up processes should be tailored to fit the organization. If management commitment exists, if employees are involved and clarify why they feel the way they do, if employees receive communication regarding the resultant action plans, and if the survey process is viewed as ongoing, then the effectiveness of survey feedback organization development as a change strategy is virtually assured.

The results of employee opinion surveys and survey feedback are mirror images of an organization's commitment to the process. The reflection is always clear, especially to employees.

Chapter Eight

Setting Goals for Improvements in Survey Results

Three things about the setting of improvement goals are known: organizations that set goals outperform those that don't, those that set specific goals outperform those that set general goals, and those that set difficult goals outperform those that set easy goals.

In this chapter, I review three topics that will help organizations with their goal setting, allowing them to achieve the highest return on investment from their survey feedback and action planning processes. The first topic is about establishing guidelines for what represents a practically significant change in actual results between successive administrations of a survey. The second focuses on the gap closure method of goal setting, a process especially relevant to the setting of intermediate goals within the context of an organization that is pursuing mid- to long-term strategies. The final topic introduces the behavior change index, which is embedded in a broader methodology that helps organizations stay on track in the use of employee survey results and in the achievement of the feedback and action planning goals. The focus in this chapter is on how to think about goal setting, not on a prescriptive systematic guide to the setting of survey results–based improvement goals.

Practically Significant Changes in Survey Results

Being effective in establishing survey-based change goals assumes knowledge regarding what represents a practically significant difference in survey results over successive measurements. Whether the results being compared are dimension or item scores, differences can be computed and subjected to statistical testing to determine if the difference is statistically significant. That approach may prove successful, but only for a slim portion of the total population of managers. It assumes that managers have a good working knowledge of how to use tests of significant differences.

For the vast majority of managers, there is a notably simpler approach. This approach is based on statistical principles but does not require the testing of differences for every potential comparison of survey results over time:

If number of respondents in the unit compared is . . .	Look for differences in percentage favorable of . . .
One hundred or more	5 percent or more
Fifty to ninety-nine	10 percent or more
Fewer than fifty	15 percent or more

Early in my career, I developed these guidelines, which are straightforward and emphasize that determining whether a difference in survey results across periods is significant depends on the size of the organization or unit being compared. If the organization or a unit within the organization exceeds one hundred survey respondents in size, a five percentage point difference represents a "practically" significant difference. For smaller organizational units, larger differences are needed to conclude that the change over time is practically significant. It is in this respect that the guidelines follow basic statistical principles. Just as with a statistical test, unit size is considered in determining the threshold for a significant difference. This stands to reason. In a smaller group of respondents, the change in opinion of just a few people can have a dramatic impact on the computation of the score for that unit. Thus, the smaller the group is, the larger the difference is required in order to conclude that the difference is both reliable and practically significant.

Determining whether a difference in survey results across periods is significant depends on the size of the organization or unit being compared.

When comparing the conclusions reached by adopting these guidelines with the conclusions reached from actual statistical tests of significant differences, I found the guidelines mimicked the results of statistical testing 90 percent of the time. In the spirit of helping managers actually get on with the use of survey results, these guidelines have proven invaluable. Instead of wasting time and energy over what constitutes a statistically significant difference, the guidelines illuminate the path to a more efficient decision-making process.

The upshot of all of this is that managers who want to improve scores on the next survey by a significant margin should target a five percentage point improvement as their minimal goal. Although in some cases that may seem like a low hurdle, the idea is that over multiple administrations of the survey, the improvements accumulate. In a three-year period, for example, successive five-point improvements will total fifteen percentage points in improvement. As I discuss in the next chapter, compounded improvements over a longer time frame is the real goal. When such improvements build on one another over a longer period, they became more substantial and are less easily shaken by minor events or lesser temporary influences.

As with most other guidelines, a couple of points (or limitations) need to be mentioned. First, the guidelines were developed with a unit manager in mind. In other words, they are aimed at helping managers review results specific to their respective organizational units, or even for executives reviewing the results for total organizations that are relatively smaller in size (that is, organizations with one thousand to twenty-five hundred respondents). Clearly, for executives of very large organizations (fifty thousand or more respondents), the guidelines require modification. The threshold to establish a practically significant difference lowers when examining scores over successive administrations for such massive organizations. In such cases, changes of three to four percentage points in favorability represent practically significant differences (assuming survey response rates are sufficiently high to be representative of the total organization).

Second, the guidelines were developed primarily for comparison of scores over time to individual survey questions. Because dimension scores comprise the scores to several individual survey questions, they are inherently more reliable. With this more reliable measurement, the threshold for establishing significant differences also lowers, especially as organizational size increases. In cases of an organizational size of five thousand or more respondents and when reviewing dimension level scores, changes of three to four percentage points in favorability represent practically significant differences (again, assuming survey response rates are sufficiently high to be representative of the organization).

The Gap Closure Method for Goal Setting

The gap closure method can be a powerful tool in establishing goals for future survey results. In my experience, it works best for larger organizations that are focused on a few key dimension or index scores that they want to improve over the course of a longer period, for example, five to ten years. The method itself is borrowed from the statistical quality control and reengineering movements. The idea is simple: define a desired state, and work incrementally to achieve that desired state within a specified time frame. Let me illustrate by way of an example:

I worked with a major global manufacturing and services organization. The organization had undertaken a rigorous strategic planning process aimed at identifying the type of organization it would need to be in order to meet its ten-year strategic objectives. The human resource strategy, built to support its overall business strategy, called for a significant upgrade of across-the-organization leadership skills. Thus, the scores on the leadership effectiveness and employee engagement indexes emerged as critical measures of plan progress. (Leadership effectiveness measures the extent to which employees view their leaders as carrying out their leadership responsibilities effectively.) The organization conducts a census survey every year. Despite significant improvements on both indexes from year 1 to year 2 of its survey, both index scores were still below the fiftieth percentile of the normative database after year 2.

This client determined that within five years, it wanted to be at the seventy-fifth percentile of scores for comparable organizations within the normative database. These were indeed lofty goals, especially for an organization with well over one hundred thousand employees worldwide. The results were at 56 percent favorable on the employee engagement index, and the seventy-fifth percentile threshold was 74 percent favorable. It was at 55 percent favorable on the leadership effectiveness index, and the seventy-fifth percentile threshold was 73 percent favorable. For both indexes, it needed to improve by eighteen percentage points in five years, assuming no change in the thresholds over that time frame.

In consultation with this client's leadership team, we decided to use the gap closure method but with some modifications. In its simplest form, the method would involve dividing the gap (eighteen percentage points) by the number of "periods" (five years). This would mean improving the scores by an average of 3.6 points in favorability for five successive years. The discussions led to a review of strategic priorities and resource availability. In the end, we determined that for the next three years, the client would target improvements of roughly four percentage points per year. At the end of that time, it would target increases of three percentage points per year until the target was reached and exceeded.

The goals (targeted survey scores) established through this modified gap closure method were approved by the leadership team. The CEO was new and had come up from within the ranks of an organization that had a consistent history of long-tenured CEOs. Thus, he expected to be in his position during the time frame contemplated by these targets. In addition, the goal of achieving the seventy-fifth percentile threshold on both key indexes would still be achieved within the broader context of the overall ten-year strategic plan that initially set all of these plans and measures in motion. The year-by-year targets also reflected the reality that larger improvements in survey scores would be more achievable in the early years, especially given the organization's starting point of being well below the fiftieth percentile at the time of measurement. The leadership team members acknowledged that as they improved their relative position versus the scores of other organizations, the latter improvements would be harder to achieve. Finally, we agreed that sustained and consistent growth was the most desirable. They wanted to avoid the temptation to set seemingly unachievable stretch goals that might cause wild swings in year-over-year results as managers and executives attempted to maintain balance in their overall responsibilities and deliver against the various metrics toward which they were managing.

The gap closure method is a legitimate way—and, in fact, a powerful tool—for establishing longer-range targets for improvements in survey scores. It uses techniques proven successful in other fields of organizational improvement and helps executives be more realistic in their goal-setting processes, particularly with regard to needed time frames for target achievement. As this example shows, the method itself may need to be adjusted slightly to fit the circumstances and reflect other influences and realities. These adjustments are appropriate when they serve to make goals more compatible with other strategic objectives and more acceptable to managers responsible for their achievement.

The Behavior Change Index Methodology

The behavior change index (BCI) methodology was created to help organizations achieve their targeted survey improvement goals. The methodology allows an organization to gauge the success of its action planning efforts and create more accountability among executives and managers for following up on and using survey results to bring about desired changes.

Although the index takes on different forms to fit different client settings, most typically it measures whether the results to a previous survey were shared and discussed and whether responsive actions were implemented at both local and higher levels within the organization. The most typical behavior change index items are:

- Were the results of the survey communicated to my group?
- Was I given the opportunity to discuss my questions and ideas about the results of the survey?
- Has my manager taken action based on the feedback from the employee survey?
- Has the executive leadership of the organization taken action based on the feedback from the employee survey?

In practice, the BCI methodology may be embedded in a pulse survey taken between administrations of a major survey program or, more typically, be included as part of that major survey effort. In this respect, the BCI is applicable only for organizations that have already established a survey program and are at least in the second iteration of measurement. Organizations that are struggling to build accountability for action are especially attracted to the methodology. By clear implication, the BCI is not relevant when the purposes of the survey do not include sharing results and taking action against them.

I have learned from experience that organizations must have realistic expectations about their effectiveness in using survey results. I counsel clients that the main goal for the first year of surveying is to build trust and confidence in the overall process. Ultimately survey feedback and action planning success boils down to the quality of follow-through at the local level. In most organizations, 30 percent of managers will move ahead with sharing results and building actions with little or no direction; another 30 percent want to take action but need direction and guidance; another 30 percent are resistant to the survey feedback and action planning processes and would rather focus on harder business metrics, and these are the ones most in need of being held accountable; and the final 10 percent of managers will do nothing. This last group typically is ineffective in carrying out most managerial responsibilities and thus is a drag on overall organizational success.

The main goal for the first year of surveying is to build trust and confidence in the overall process.

Many client organizations have successfully implemented the BCI methodology. They find it helpful because it raises levels of commitment and personal accountability for following up on survey results and implementing action plans at both the executive and managerial levels. Obviously it is the reporting of results on the BCI that creates a feedback loop facilitating self-improvement. In reality, and almost without exception, groups scoring the highest on the BCI concomitantly demonstrate the largest improvements on such basic measures as the employee engagement index. Figure 8.1 shows the relationship between a

Figure 8.1 Managers Acting on Survey Results and Employee Engagement Levels

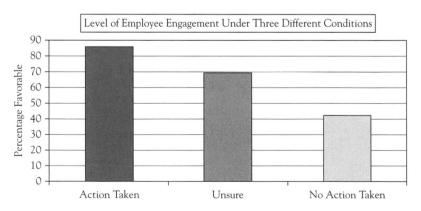

Level of Employee Engagement Under Three Different Conditions

belief that one's manager acted on the previous set of survey results and the current level of employee engagement. The EEI for units whose managers acted on survey results is more than twice that of those units whose managers took no action.

From an aspirational perspective, the goal of the organization should be that all of its employees believe they are sharing, discussing, and taking action on survey results. Not surprisingly, client experiences are substantially different from that (see Table 8.1). These results indicate that for most organizations, about two-thirds of employees report that survey results have been shared with them, and slightly less than half feel that follow-up actions have been taken. Organizations that fall into the top quartile on BCI scores fare much better. For those organizations, four of every five employees agree that survey results have been shared, and almost two-thirds report that responsive actions have been taken. These data are based on more than thirty projects. There is great confidence in the actual item scores because they are based on cumulative responses of between 280,000 and 830,000 employees, depending on the item under consideration.

Although these numbers are telling, often such normative data will not be included in client reports. The fear is that such information may give executives and managers a reason

Table 8.1 Normative Scores for the Behavior Change Index

Behavior Change Index	Percentage Favorable	
	All Projects	Top Quartile[a]
Index score	55	71
Items	—	—
1. Survey results communicated	65	83
2. Survey results discussed	58	70
3. Manager acted on results	49	65
4. Leadership acted on results	47	64

[a]Average for organizations whose BCI results place them in the top quartile of BCI scores.

Figure 8.2 Effective Survey Feedback and Action Planning and Improvements in Employee Engagement

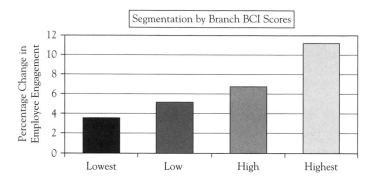

or excuse not to follow through. Focusing on ensuring that managers understand the relationship between effective follow-through and organization change and improvement is far more important. Figure 8.2 provides another client-based example. For this analysis, branches of a transportation organization were categorized into four segments based on their BCI scores. The figure clearly indicates the relationship between effective survey feedback and action planning processes and improvements in employee engagement.

In the final analysis, the BCI methodology is about change management. Its value is in helping organizations and their executives and managers overcome obstacles to change. It positions organizations to recognize and reward those who are effective in their survey feedback and follow-up practices. It allows organizations to publish and promote the experiences of those who are effective as learning opportunities for those in need of coaching. And it contributes to the positive use of survey results as a platform for organization development and helps organizations achieve their survey-based improvement goals.

> *The BCI methodology is about change management.*

Summary

This chapter is about setting improvement goals for subsequent administrations of an employee survey. Reviewed in this chapter are three ideas. The first idea deals with identifying the threshold of a practically significant difference between survey results over two periods. For most organizations, a five percentage point improvement represents the threshold of a practically significant difference and is therefore a meaningful change goal. The second idea deals with a methodology for setting goals over a longer period, for example, five to ten years. In those circumstances, the gap closure method is valuable. In implementing the method, a desired state is defined, and then the organization works in incremental steps to achieve that desired state; the method specifies the time frame by which the longer-term goal will be reached. The third idea is a methodology for managing change. The methodology, which employs a behavior change index, involves holding managers accountable for achieving change goals. Experience shows that managers who review and discuss survey results with employees, and then implement actions based on survey results, significantly improve employee engagement levels.

Chapter Nine

Sustaining Change

Once an organization has achieved positive change in survey results from one measurement to the next, it faces the challenge of sustaining change over an extended time frame. Since the way survey programs are viewed in an organization is largely influenced by how they are handled by the organization's leaders, internal practitioners want to understand the mind-set or belief systems of leadership teams whose overall organizational employee survey scores improve with each administration. From my experience, leadership teams whose organizations continuously improve have the characteristics set out in the rest of this chapter.

They have a clearly articulated vision, mission, and value system.

A characteristic of best practice organizations is that they clearly communicate to employees their mission, vision, and values (Becker and Gerhart, 1996). This benefits employees in a number of ways:

- It tells them what is important to their employer, the behavior they are expected to demonstrate, and what they can expect from leadership.
- It indicates the direction in which the organization is headed and why—how it will compete in the marketplace and differentiate itself from others.
- It helps create employee alignment and commitment to the organization, especially if leadership acts with integrity in pursuit of the organization's mission.

The employee survey instrument itself can be designed to measure the organization's progress on elements of its mission, vision, and values. This is exactly what happened with one of my clients, a global manufacturing organization. It not only had clearly articulated mission, vision, and values statements, but it also had communicated to its employees the strategy for achieving the mission. Thus, all dimensions of the survey could be linked to mission, vision, values, or strategy. In the very communication of the survey to employees, the leaders emphasized the key reason for the survey program: to measure progress on effectively implementing the mission, vision, values, and strategy. Indirectly, it also gave the organization one more opportunity to reinforce to employees where it was headed and what it needed from managers and employees to achieve its goals.

The employee survey instrument itself can be designed to measure the organization's progress on elements of its mission, vision, and values.

The essence of this point is survey design. If the survey measures what is important to the organization, the actual survey results will point the leadership team to the right survey follow-up priorities—that is, the priorities that most support the goals. In the example, the organization understood, in advance of the first survey, that it needed to upgrade its leadership and supervisory skills and resources. Understanding the need, a leadership effectiveness index was included in the survey to measure the current quality of leadership and supervision. Once the survey results database was assembled, an analysis was conducted to identify the drivers of leadership effectiveness. The organization then designed its action plans to address these drivers. Because of this dedication and discipline, the results of their subsequent surveys showed marked improvement.

They believe in performance management—that is, holding executive and managerial staff accountable.

Organizations undertake employee survey programs for different reasons. In the final analysis, though, most reasons boil down to the belief that the survey results (once described to me by a CEO of a leading global medical products manufacturer as an organizational asset) form the foundation for change and organization development. Results of an employee survey do indeed represent an asset, but creating that asset takes significant investments of time, energy, and financial resources. In most cases, there is a tangible cost, assuming the organization uses an outside provider, as most large organizations do. In all cases, there are internal costs, including management time to create and oversee the survey program and employee time to take the survey and help management sort through the results and planned actions. Given this investment, it makes sense that the organization and its leadership should act with urgency in ensuring the asset is well deployed.

Organizations that fail to sustain improvement in employee survey results from year to year tend to share one common feature: they fail to hold those executives and managers who receive reports of survey results accountable. In this context, *accountability* means fundamentally that managers will invest the time and energy to understand the profile of their results— the strengths as well as the opportunities for improvement. That is the foundation of moving forward. More important, accountability means that managers will communicate the survey results to their employees, develop and implement action plans to address areas of priority, and keep employees informed of actions taken and their consequences. The bottom line is that organizations must hold managers accountable for survey follow-up in order to achieve improvement that is sustained over time.

At the very least, higher-level managers should, at the time of performance evaluation, take into consideration how effectively the subordinate manager followed up on the most recent survey (see the discussion in Chapter Eight on the behavior change index methodology). My counsel is not to overly focus on the absolute survey scores or how they compare to an internal or external norm, but to place the attention more properly on the quality of the response to the results. That takes time and energy on the part of higher-level managers; it is also what produces the most potent outcomes. Quarterly one-on-one performance reviews or even more public operational reviews are an excellent time for leadership to assess progress. Should bonus plans be established to reward managers who show progress on survey scores? Maybe—but that can also be a slippery slope.

Managers must have control and influence over the desired outcome and the behaviors that produce that outcome in order for a bonus to have its desired effect. That should be a given in the selection of priorities for follow-up, but it is not always the case. (For example, in most cases, lower-level managers should not select policy-level issues as their action areas; they are often too far removed to address those directly.) In addition, organizations must be wary of managers' gaming the system to ensure maximum bonus payout. Clearly the quality of survey follow-up will be reflected in the results of the next survey; in many respects, that is the decisive test. Between surveys, though, the focus of organizational leadership should be on ensuring that managers communicate results to employees, develop and implement high-quality action plans, and keep their employees informed of progress.

They understand the employee-customer-performance dynamic— that customer and business results are delivered through people, and their performance correlates with how they are led.

For thirty years, the literature in the science of industrial-organizational psychology has shown a direct relationship of how employees describe the quality of their work environment, how satisfied customers are with the products and services derived from that work environment, and the business performance achieved through that work environment. (For summaries of these research findings, see Wiley, 1996; Wiley and Brooks, 2000; and Brooks, Wiley, and Hause, 2006.) Others sometimes present this dynamic as "happy employees make for happy customers who make for happy investors." This is both overly simplistic and misleading—misleading because it implies that the goal of workforce management is to produce happy workers and sets in course all manner of action plans that will have nothing to do with achieving high performance.

As noted in Chapter Six, having both a high-performance organization and an engaged workforce are complementary goals, the achievement of which has its roots in the requirements inherent in effective leadership. A high-performance organization is a result of leadership practices that stress customer orientation, place an emphasis on product and service quality, ensure the proper training of employees, and involve employees in decisions that affect their work. Employee engagement results when leaders and managers inspire employee trust and confidence; provide recognition, respect, and opportunities for growth and development; and match the work to the abilities and interests of employees.

The validation of the High Performance–Engagement Model in Chapter Six demonstrates the additive and interactive effects of stressing both performance excellence and employee engagement, thereby positioning employees to deliver the optimal results for the organization. This is a much more nuanced understanding of employee motivation and performance than the simple paradigm that happy employees lead to happy customers and therefore happy investors. Leadership teams that sustain improvements in survey results over successive administrations understand this more complex picture of organizational performance.

They faithfully measure what matters and share the results with staff.

A number of things can matter to an organization. First, this refers to measuring things that lend themselves to valid and reliable measurement using an employee survey and link to mission, vision, values, strategy, or business outcomes. A survey effectively designed can do both.

It also refers to the notion of a consistent measurement process—one that managers and employees come to expect and that has been explained in terms of the values it provides the organization. Most likely, this measurement occurs on a given cycle— one for which there is an organizational rhythm. Such a process is not viewed as an extra task heaped on the backs of already overburdened managers, but as an important part of "how we conduct our business." Organizations that are the best in sustaining change over time develop survey programs viewed and handled in this way.

They also do something else. They are dedicated to sharing results with the staff. Executives and managers are held accountable. These are not organizations where employees are left wondering for one, two, three, or more months as to whatever became of the survey they took. Managers in these organizations have learned how to interpret results, feed them back to employees, and inject employee input into the development of responsive action plans. In addition, they keep employees informed regarding the organization's progress in implementing action plans.

Several years ago, I worked with a large natural resources organization that was ready to go into the second cycle of its survey program. I spoke to a number of employees about the success of the first survey cycle, looking for ways to improve the process. I was surprised to learn that a number of employees had not heard about what (if anything) had happened with the results. Yes, they were aware of the survey results, but had no clue what actions were implemented to address the established priorities. This taught me an early lesson about the importance of organizations' "merchandising" the actions taken because of a previous survey. Organizations must make the effort to let employees know how their input is being used to bring about change. Not only does this build alignment and engagement, it also has the natural consequence of keeping employee survey participation rates high because employees have faith that their voice is being heard and that what they say is valued.

> *Organizations must make the effort to let employees know how their input is being used to bring about change.*

They have persistence.

This may be the most important lesson learned about sustaining change. It may also be the most obvious because sustained improvement demands persistence. Fundamentally, persistence has to do with continuing a course of action in spite of change or interference. Organizations that have outperformed their cohorts on sustaining improvements in survey results are those whose leadership is persistent in using employee input and observations as a primary foundation of organization development.

One of my clients is the very model of persistence. More than twenty years ago, a survey measuring its articulated mission, vision, values, and strategy was designed. Linkage research demonstrated that its employee survey results potently predicted customer satisfaction and retention, which predicted improvements in sales and net income. This validated the survey program and gave management a clear agenda for the changes most needed to sustain further improvement. The instrument and overall program have evolved over the years as the needs of the organization have changed. The program has survived the organization's being sold as well as acquiring several competitors. Through all of this, the leadership, now in its third generation, remains fully committed to the employee survey process. For the past ten years, this organization has dominated the North American market in which it competes. Every member of its current leadership team would state that the survey program, and the insight it provides, has been a key element in its achievement of market domination.

There are two major threats to persistence: distraction by external conditions and overconfidence. The first threat has to do with changes in the external marketplace that create competition for the use of the resources necessary to sustain the survey program. These changes may be due to increased or new competition, regulation, declines in demand, or economic crises. The second threat has to do with a sense that develops within the organization's leadership that current results are "okay," perhaps comparable to available norms, and therefore don't represent a mandate for change. The threat of being overly confident can also arise from having achieved improvement in results from time 1 to time 2, and therefore leadership begins backpedaling from the initial commitment to survey employees regularly.

Summary

Continuous improvement will position organizations to be more capable in the competitive space in which they operate. The common theme among the characteristics of leadership teams whose organizational survey scores improve from year to year is commitment. This commitment encompasses ensuring that workers understand the organization's value system, holding managers accountable for following up on survey results, understanding it is their employees who deliver the customer value proposition, making sure employees are aware of the action plans in place from the latest survey, and persisting in their belief, despite change or interference, that employee input is a critical piece of building a top-notch organization and becoming truly an employer of choice.

The common theme among the characteristics of leadership teams whose organizational survey scores improve from year to year is commitment.

Chapter Ten

Final Thoughts

From experience, I have learned that two things most differentiate successful and unsuccessful employee survey programs. The first has to do with asking the right questions—questions that produce results important to the leadership of the organization. Part One of this book addresses this issue. The second has to with establishing a plan, in advance, for how survey results are going to be used. I am not simply referencing how results to an initial survey are going to be used, but how results are going to be used over successive measurements to effect long-lasting change. Part Two of this book addresses this issue.

This chapter summarizes the book and introduces two new thoughts: one derived from common sense and one derived from data yet to be reviewed.

Summary of Part One

Conducting employee surveys is neither new nor uncommon in organizations today, particularly larger organizations. One of the primary theses of this book is contained in Part One: in order to maximize the effectiveness of an employee survey program, the program must be strategic, that is, important to the completion of a strategic plan or of great importance to an integrated or planned effort. In other words, survey programs produce their greatest return on investment for organizations when they are consciously part of an organization's business strategy. When survey programs are embedded in business strategy, decisions about what to measure, when to measure, and how to use that measurement for greatest gain will be much easier to make.

I introduced the Strategic Survey Model in Chapter One. The model summarizes my views of why organizations conduct

Figure 10.1 The Strategic Survey Model

Copyright © Kenexa 2010

employee surveys. These reasons can be placed on a continuum of defensive to offensive reasons as depicted by Figure 10.1. The four reasons, which may overlap within the context of a single program, are:

1. To identify warning signs of trouble within the organization
2. To evaluate the effectiveness of specific programs, policies, and initiatives
3. To gauge the organization's status or strength as an employer of choice among its workforce
4. To predict and drive organizational outcomes, including customer satisfaction and business performance

A major implication of the model is that achieving a specific survey program purpose requires appropriate survey content. Chapter Two addresses using surveys as warning indicators. Examples of warning indicator type surveys are described, including surveying the topics of safety, ethics, and union vulnerability. Specific examples of appropriate survey items for these topics and typical findings are presented. Chapter Three covers using surveys as program evaluation measures. The topics of diversity and work/life balance are provided as examples, once again along with survey items and normative results. Chapters Two and Three therefore acknowledge that while surveys entirely devoted to warning indicators or program evaluation measures occur, more common is including relevant dimensions covering such topics within a longer multitopic type of survey.

> *Achieving a specific survey program purpose requires appropriate survey content.*

The most common multitopic survey conducted currently is referred to as an engagement survey. In my view, engagement surveys, reviewed in Chapter Four, are subsumed under the rubric of *employer-of-choice surveys*. In other words, most engagement surveys are conducted to understand the drivers of employee motivation and commitment to the organization; this understanding allows employers to implement responsive actions aimed at increasing motivation and commitment. In simple terms, a well-designed engagement survey will support the goals of having employees care more, perform better, and stay longer. Chapter Four provides separate analyses of retention and engagement drivers. The latter is derived from a global data set that demonstrates that engagement drivers remain largely the same across the borders of the world's major economies. This finding led to the development of a global engagement model, which was subsequently validated against measures of financial performance. This chapter also provides a generous infusion of examples of how to measure the topics of employee retention and engagement and their drivers, and what types of results these measurements typically produce.

Chapter Five shifts from surveys that treat employees as participants in an organizational system to surveys that view employees as observers and reporters of practices known to be predictive of customer satisfaction and business performance. These surveys are typified as leading indicator surveys because the organizational practices they measure have a demonstrated ability to serve as leading indicators of downstream business success. Two case studies are presented as evidence of the ability of these types of employee surveys to predict customer satisfaction and revenue growth.

Part One concludes in Chapter Six with a demonstration of how two major survey purposes, the employer-of-choice survey and the leading-indicator survey, can be merged into a single coherent survey program. Blending two robust streams of research, one focused on performance excellence and the other focused on employee engagement, the chapter introduces the new High Performance–Engagement Model. The validity of the model is demonstrated by showing how, with only eleven questions (seven comprising the performance excellence index and four comprising the employee engagement index), the model can account for almost 10 percent of diluted earnings per share across a multinational study of 158 large companies. The model and the twenty-eight attendant

Observation

Many survey instruments I review are of sufficient quality in terms of survey item development and overall questionnaire construction. The problem is that they are not assembled against clearly articulated survey purposes. This is because the inspiration behind the survey is not tied to business strategy. Such surveys are often built in copycat fashion along the lines of what other organizations are doing. The solution may not be to replace entirely the current survey. Maximum program impact may still be achievable so long as the organizers and sponsors of the survey program can show how current survey content supports both business and human resource strategy.

survey items that populate the model are put forth as an exemplar of survey impact and efficiency.

Summary of Part Two

Part Two addresses the second major differentiator between effective and ineffective survey programs: having a plan, established in advance, for how survey results will be used throughout the organization. The existence of a plan points to but does not guarantee success; however, the absence of a plan points to failure or, at the very least, diminished returns.

> *The existence of a plan points to but does not guarantee success; however, the absence of a plan points to failure or, at the very least, diminished returns.*

Chapter Seven acknowledges that organizations successful in the use of survey results to affect organization change typically follow a flow or predetermined process. The seven-step survey feedback and action planning model is introduced as an example of such a process. The model defines survey feedback as consisting of three steps: (1) understanding results, (2) establishing survey-based priorities, and (3) communicating both results and priorities to employees. Step 4 clarifies priorities by discussing with employees why they feel the way they do. In a sense, this step is both the end of the feedback part and the beginning of the action planning part of the model. The model defines the remaining steps as action planning steps: (5) generating recommendations, (6) developing and implementing action plans, and (7) monitoring progress. Chapter Seven identifies the two biggest pitfalls in implementing the model: failure to establish a short list of priorities for follow-up action planning (step 2) and failure to clarify why employees feel the way they do before generating recommendations for improvement (step 4).

Setting improvement goals is the focus of Chapter Eight. The chapter begins with a discussion of what constitutes a practically meaningful difference when comparing survey results. The answer, for most applications, is that a five percentage point difference in favorability represents a meaningful difference. The next idea reviewed is the gap closure method, a useful technique for organizations interested in establishing targeted survey goals over a longer time frame, for example, five to ten years. The idea behind this method is that of defining a desired state (the survey results goal) and working incrementally toward that goal within a specified time frame. The method is illustrated with a client case study. The final idea introduces the behavior change index methodology. This methodology, which involves surveying employees on the quality of survey feedback and action planning processes, creates more accountability among executives and managers for following up on survey results and bringing about desired changes.

The focus of Chapter Nine is sustaining improvements over time. It answers the question, "What are the characteristics of leadership teams whose survey results continuously improve over successive survey measurements?" Answering from experience, I provided five answers:

1. They understand the importance of having a clearly articulated vision, mission, and value system and want their survey instrument to align accordingly.

2. They believe in performance management and hold executive and managerial staff accountable for following up on survey results.

3. They understand the employee-customer-performance dynamic—that customer and business performance results are delivered through people and that performance correlates with how they are led.

4. They faithfully measure what matters and share the results with their staff.

5. They persist.

More Data

Before ending this book, I share one final and revealing set of data (see Table 10.1). These data report the results of a special WorkTrends analysis on global employee engagement. Unlike results I have seen reported elsewhere, these data are segmented by workers who indicate their employer has conducted an employee survey in the previous twenty-four months and those who say their employer has not. Fascinating is that the segments are equal in size: across the major economies of Brazil, Canada, China, France, Germany, India, Italy, Japan, Saudi Arabia, Russia, Spain, the United Arab Emirates, the United Kingdom, and the United States, 50 percent of employees fall into each of these two segments.

Even more fascinating is the spread in employee engagement index scores. At the overall index level, the spread is a substantial 19 percentage points. Almost two-thirds of employees whose organization has conducted a recent survey responded favorably to the items comprising the index, whereas the level of favorability among those whose organization has not recently conducted an employee survey is less than half. Among the four index items, the question dealing with advocacy—"I would

Table 10.1 Employee Engagement and Organizational Use of the Employee Survey Method

	Company Surveyed Within the Previous Twenty-Four Months			
	Overall	Yes	No	Gap
Employee engagement index	55	65	46	19
Items:				
1. Pride	58	68	49	19
2. Satisfaction	57	67	48	19
3. Advocacy	55	66	45	21
4. Retention	51	60	44	16
Percentage of respondents		50	50	

gladly refer a good friend or family member to my organization for employment"—produces the largest gap between these two segments: twenty-one percentage points.

Will conducting an employee survey give an organization a nineteen percentage point jump in the employee engagement index? Of course not; that would be a gross misapplication of these results. What these results do generally indicate, however, is that organizations that both care enough about their employees and value their input enough to ask for it have employees who are much more engaged. Their employees have more pride in their organization, are more satisfied and more committed, and are more willing to serve as an advocate for the organization.

Final Messages

The readers of this book most likely fall into two major categories: those who work in organizations that are considering conducting an employee survey and those who work in organizations that already conduct employee surveys. For both, I hope this book proves helpful. For first-timers, the key message is to understand your organization's business strategy so that program design decisions, especially those dealing with survey content, will be easier to make and prove more successful. For those already conducting surveys, the key message is that you can improve the acceptance, impact, and perceived value of your survey program by ensuring its alignment to business strategy, fine-tuning the program where needed.

References

Becker, B., and Gerhart, B. "The Impact of Human Resource Management on Organizational Performance: Progress and Prospects." *Academy of Management Journal*, 1996, 39, 779–801.

Boudreau, J. W., and Ramstad, P. M. *Beyond HR: The New Science of Human Capital*. Boston: Harvard Business School Press, 2007.

Brooks, S. M, Wiley, J. W., and Hause, E. L. "Using Employee and Customer Perspectives to Improve Organizational Performance." In L. Fogli (ed.), *Customer Service Delivery: Research and Best Practices*. San Francisco: Jossey-Bass, 2006.

Heskett, J. L., and others. "Putting the Service-Profit Chain to Work." *Harvard Business Review*, Mar.-Apr. 1994, pp. 164–174.

Higgs, A. C., and Ashworth, S. D. "Organizational Surveys: Tools for Assessment and Change." In A. I. Kraut (ed.), *Organizational Surveys*. San Francisco: Jossey-Bass, 1996.

International Monetary Fund (IMF). (2009). "World Economic Outlook Database" (data file). Available from http://www.imf.org/external/data.htm.

Kaplan, R. S., and Norton, D. P. "Using the Balanced Scorecard as a Strategic Management System." *Harvard Business Review*, 1996, 76, 75–85.

Kotter, J. O., and Heskett, J. L. *Corporate Culture and Performance*. New York: Free Press, 1992.

Kraut, A. I. "Moving the Needle: Getting Action After a Survey." In A. Kraut (ed.), *Getting Action from Organizational Surveys: New Concept, Technologies and Applications*. San Francisco: Jossey-Bass, 2006.

Rucci, A. J., Kirn, S. P., and Quinn, R. T. "The Employee-Customer-Profit Chain at Sears." *Harvard Business Review*, 1998, 76(1), 82–97.

Schiemann, W. A., and Morgan, B. S. "Strategic Surveys: Linking People to Business Strategy." In A. Kraut (ed.), *Getting Action from Organizational Surveys: New Concept, Technologies and Applications*. San Francisco: Jossey-Bass, 2006.

Schneider, B., and Bowen, D. E. "Employee and Customer Perceptions of Service in Banks: Replication and Extension." *Journal of Applied Psychology*, 1985, 70, 423–433.

Schneider, B., Parkington, J. J., and Buxton, V. M. "Employee and Customer Perceptions of Service in Banks." *Administrative Science Quarterly*, 1980, *25*, 252–267.

TalentKeepers. "Turnover Cost Calculator." June 2005. http://www.talentkeepers-services.com/talentkeepers/costcalc.asp.

Wiley, J. W. "Making the Most of Survey Feedback as a Strategy for Organization Development." *OD Practitioner*, 1991, *23*(1), 1–4.

Wiley, J. W. "Linking Survey Results to Customer Satisfaction and Business Performance." In A. Kraut (ed.), *Organizational Surveys: Tools for Assessment and Change*. San Francisco: Jossey-Bass, 1996.

Wiley, J. W. "The Strategic Employee Survey." In R. J. Burke and C. L. Cooper (Ed.), *The Human Resources Revolution: Why Putting People First Matters*. Amsterdam: Elsevier, 2006.

Wiley, J. W., and Brooks, S. M. "The High-Performance Organizational Climate: How Workers Describe Top Performing Units." In N. S. Ashkanasy, C. Wilderom, and M. F. Peterson (eds.), *The Handbook of Organizational Culture and Climate*. Thousand Oaks, Calif.: Sage, 2000.

Wiley, J. W., and Campbell, B. H. "Using Linkage Research to Drive High Performance." In A. Kraut (ed.), *Getting Action from Organizational Surveys: New Concept, Technologies and Applications*. San Francisco: Jossey-Bass, 2006.

Wiley, J. W., and Weiner, S. P. "Driving Organizational Outcomes with Strategic Employee Surveys: Best Practices from Internal and External Perspectives." Workshop at the Seventeenth Annual Conference of the Society for Industrial and Organizational Psychology, Toronto, Ontario, Apr. 2002.

Index

Page references followed by *fig* indicate an illustrated figure; followed by *t* indicate a table.